IMAGES
OF LEEDS
1850~1960

IMAGES OF LEEDS
1850~1960

PETER BREARS

BREEDON
BOOKS

First published in Great Britain by
The Breedon Books Publishing Company Limited
44 Friar Gate, Derby DE1 1DA
1992

ISBN 1 873626 06 1

Printed and bound in Great Britain by
Butler & Tanner Ltd, Frome and London.
Jacket printed by BDC Printing Services Ltd of Derby.

Contents

Foreword

OVER the past 170 years, the Leeds Museums have collected, studied and preserved around one million specimens of local and international interest for the benefit of the people of Leeds and its region. Many are seen by the 350,000 or more visitors who come to enjoy the Museum's exhibitions each year, or are studied by researchers from Europe and beyond. Even so, the majority of the collections remain in store for long periods, out of public view.

I am very pleased that this book will now make a major part of the collection of local photographs permanently accessible to everyone who has an interest in the history of Leeds. There is something for everyone, including views of the fine historic buildings, the street scenes, transport systems, industries, housing, entertainments and events which played such an important part in the life and work of Leeds people between 1850 and 1960.

On behalf of the Museums Sub-Committee, and the City Council, I hope that this book will add to your enjoyment and appreciation of our great city.

Councillor Mrs C.Myers
Chairman
May 1992

Introduction and Acknowledgements

ALTHOUGH archaeological and historical records show that people have lived around the Leeds area for over 2,000 years, it was not until around 1700 that the first view of the town was drawn. William Lodge's engraving shows Leeds as a largely half-timbered and brick-built country town, with cattle grazing on the tenter-fields which ran down to the crystal-clear River Aire. Similar prospects taken in the eighteenth century show it prospering as the elegant centre of the world's greatest market in woollen cloth, with fine new churches, cloth halls, and merchants' mansions. By 1842, when Samuel Topham set up the first photographic gallery here, the scene had changed almost beyond recognition, as Leeds had developed into a booming industrial centre, with numerous textile, engineering, leather and pottery factories.

Over the period 1850-1960, thousands of photographs of Leeds were taken both by highly-skilled amateurs, such as the members of the Leeds Photographic Society, founded in 1852, and by a number of excellent professional photographers. Some of their work was undertaken for aesthetic reasons, such as the carefully composed views of Kirkstall Abbey, etc. whilst still more was taken in order to record the historic fabric of the town, including its oldest and most interesting buildings, before they were swept away for redevelopment. Care was also taken to record important events in the town's history, such as the building of the Town Hall, Royal visits, great parades, the opening of City Square, etc. so that they could be enjoyed by future generations of Leeds people.

Photography was similarly used to record the Corporation's great achievement in transforming the whole appearance and condition of Leeds during this period. The insanitary yards of old back-to-back houses, cellar-dwellings, and privy-middens ridden with cholera, typhus and other evils were all photographed to provide evidence for the Improvement Acts which enabled them to be demolished. The photographers then returned later to record the new blocks of houses, flats or shops which soon rose in their place. In the same way, the narrow lanes of Leeds, which still retained their original medieval dimensions, were all carefully photographed before being demolished in order to create fine broad thoroughfares such as Boar Lane or The Headrow, which form such a major feature of the modern city.

As Leeds developed as a great manufacturing centre, professional photographers including the Wormald family and Charles R.H.Pickard, 'The Business Photographer', were employed to photograph the interiors and exteriors of the massive factories which grew up here, thus establishing an invaluable record of the working life of the community. They also photographed the major products as they stood in pristine condition in the works yards, ready for despatch to customers located in virtually every part of the world. Today these pictures form a unique testimony to the high quality of innovative design, skill and efficiency which gave Leeds' products such an enviable international reputation.

Leeds City Museum acquired its first photographs in 1856, and since that time it has built up a collection of many thousands of images covering various aspects of human and natural life both in this country and overseas. The majority of the photographs in this volume come from this source, and I am grateful to Mr & Mrs Ken and Rita Booth of York, Mr Peter Wilson and Mr George Wilson of the Friends of the City Museums, and Mr Mike Hargreaves of New Dimension Photography for preparing the copy prints required. A further group of photographs have been taken from the unique collections housed in the City's Local and Family History Library. Sincere thanks are due to Mrs Ann Heap for her usual help and efficiency in providing ready access to the material there, and to Mr David Sheard for his excellent photography. In addition, I would also like to thank Mr Dudley Mitchell of Joshua Tetley & Son for providing the photograph of the brewery on page 166, the University of Reading, Institute of Agricultural History and Museum of English Rural Life, for the photograph of the John Fowler ploughing engine on page 160, Mr Bill Connor of the West Yorkshire Archive Service for the photographs of the Hathorn Davey Foundry on page 165 and Mr A.Wells-Cole of Temple Newsam House for the photographs on pages 176-7, and also Yorkshire Post Newspapers. Sincere thanks are also due to Mrs Gill Philipson, the City Museum's secretary, for typing the numerous captions.

Since effective colour photography was only in relatively limited use between 1850 and 1960, the colour plates in this book have all been taken from original works of art in the City Museum. It is the first time that most of them have appeared in print, but they certainly help to give a rich impression of how the town looked during the Victorian and Edwardian periods.

It is hoped that all those who know Leeds well will enjoy being reminded of its appearance over thirty years ago, before any of the recent developments had taken place, before its buildings were cleaned and when it still lay beneath a permanent pall of black smoke. For those who are new here, this book should also provide a useful introduction to Leeds, helping to explain how it developed into its present form as 'England's Northern Capital', and one of Britain's most interesting cities.

Peter Brears,
Leeds City Museum
April 1992

It is entirely appropriate that the first illustration in this book should be one of the earliest landscape photographs taken in Leeds, and that its subject should be one of the city's earliest buildings. Kirkstall Abbey was built by monks of the Cistercian order between 1152 and 1182, most of this original structure still surviving up to roof level to make it the most complete early monastic ruin in Britain. This photograph of the east end of the church was taken in 1852, shortly after a programme of essential repairs had been carried out by the Beecroft and Butler families of Kirkstall Forge. The cross-shaped iron ties they inserted can be seen at the eaves of the central gable, while their new wall at the bottom of the great east window blocked a roadway up the valley which had been in use for some two hundred years.

Abbey House, the great gatehouse of Kirkstall Abbey was the only part of the buildings to continue in domestic use after the dissolution of the monastery in 1539. At that time the five-light window seen here was inserted in the original twelfth-century gateway, to make a ground-floor living area, while the thirteenth-century chapel above was converted into bedrooms. Having served as a farmhouse for three hundred years, the gatehouse was transformed into a fashionable residence in 1841 by George Skirrow Beecroft, leading partner at the nearby Kirkstall Forge. Further extensions in the Gothic style were made by John Octavius Butler, another partner at the forge, in 1870, this photograph probably being taken at that time to record his work. The pinnacle on the roof bears his initials 'J.O.B. 1870'.

Here, beneath the rib-vaulted ceiling of the great gatehouse at Kirkstall, brown-robed lay brothers, feudal barons and their retainers, and other visitors, waited for the gates to swing back to grant them access to the inner precinct with its fine church and surrounding buildings. This photograph shows the gate porch as it appeared around 1870, when it served as John Octavius Butler's dining room. The furniture is typical of the period, with sideboard, side table, dining table and chairs all carved in elaborate 'Jacobean' oak.

Stank Hall Barn at Beeston is an impressive manorial structure built to hold hay and corn in the fifteenth century. At a later date accommodation for cattle was added to its lower end, while in the seventeenth century its upper end was extended by a fine masonry stable block, with probable living areas for farm staff on its upper floors. It remained in agricultural use up to the 1960s, but then its condition began to cause some concern, all the major local archaeological societies making a joint appeal for its preservation in 1973. A proposal to convert it into a restaurant brought fresh fears for its future, and so the City Council carried out a full restoration of the fabric in 1987-88. This was so successful that the scheme won the Leeds Award for Architecture in 1991.

Richard Sykes, a leading inhabitant of Leeds in the reign of James I, built this fine timber-framed house on Briggate in 1615, his initials and the date being recorded on the small plaque just above the sign-board. By the time that this photograph was taken in 1900 someone had carved away part of the '6' to make it a '5', thus adding a further spurious century to its age. Regrettably it was demolished for extensions to Timpson's Shoe Shop in 1955, but an entry at the side still leads into Pack Horse Yard.

Lambert's Yard, just off Lower Briggate, takes its name from a family of grocers who traded here in the early nineteenth century. At first it appears to have little or no architectural interest, but in fact it includes one of the oldest houses left in the city. The three-storey gabled building in the corner is completely timber-framed, and probably formed part of a larger house built here around the opening years of the seventeenth century.

The Knights Templar acquired the manor of Newsam in 1155, thus giving the title of Temple Newsam to the large estate on the eastern outskirts of Leeds, and more particularly to its great country house, built by Thomas Davey in the early sixteenth century. After centuries of ownership by the Ingram family, Viscounts Irwin, it was purchased by the City of Leeds in 1922. Since that time it has been developed as one of Britain's finest museums of decorative art, displaying outstanding collections of furniture, pottery and silverware.

Today the iron railings have disappeared, as has its centrepiece, a shell weighing 26cwt which was cast at the Low Moor Iron Works for the Crimean War, and presented to Hugo Maynell in 1856.

Standing in Killingbeck, not far from the railway embankment just before Cross Gates Station, this sixteenth and seventeenth-century cottage was first recorded as the house of William Thompson in 1638. Then, on 8 January 1722, it was advertised as being 'to lett for a term of years from Candlemas next', along with barns, outhouse, and thirty acres of pasture, suitable for 'if two or three clothiers are minded to joyne at the whole (the owner) is willing to make suitable conveyances'.

Unfortunately this fine building did not survive the first half of the twentieth century, being demolished in 1949.

Wade Hall stood between Woodhouse Lane and Wade Lane in the area of the present Merrion Centre. It was built about 1630-40 by Thomas Jackson, with a panelled and studded oak door, rooms clad in fine oak panelling with friezes richly carved in foliage and grotesque heads, and decorative plaster ceilings. In 1863, following the sale of the property, the majority of its massive structure was demolished, some of the panelling being removed to Moor House, Headingley. The remaining portion was then converted into the Old Hall Hotel, as we see in this photograph of around 1900. The left-hand façade is an interior wall refaced in the 1860s, that to the right being original work of the 1630s.

Knostrop Hall, one of the finest late seventeenth-century mansions in the Leeds area, was built by Adam Baynes (1620-1670), 'Parliament man for Leeds' during the Commonwealth, and the town's only MP until the Reform Bill of 1832. Designed for show, the visitor passed between these ornate gate-piers with their contemporary seats, along a diamond-paved path up to the porch, and then into the hall, at one end of which stood a table raised on a high dais. Around 1880 the famous Leeds artist Atkinson Grimshaw took up residence here, but, after his death, it was occupied by a variety of tennants until its demolition in 1960.

This remarkably complete seventeenth-century bathhouse still stands intact in Gledhow Valley woods. The large stone in the right-hand wall bears a Latin inscription informing us that it was built by Edward Waddington of Gledhow in 1671. Ralph Thoresby describes it as 'a very curious cold spring, which in a Romish Country could not have miss'd the Patronage of some noted Saint: Tis of late years accommodated with convenient Lodgings to sweat the Patient after Bathing, and is frequented by persons of Honour, being reputed little or nothing inferior of St Mongah's.'

Inside Knostrop Hall, the quality of the woodwork and plasterwork was of the highest standard. Here we see the carved oak overmantle of the fireplace. The shield between the left-hand dragons has a pair of crossed shin bones, the arms of the Baynes family granted in 1650, while that on the right, with a stag in one corner, has the arms of Dawson, representing Adam Baynes' wife, Martha Dawson of Heworth.

No.10, Town End was built some time before 1725 for Robert Denison, and was subsequently owned by the Sheepshanks family. Constructed of brick with stone dressings, it provides an excellent example of a Leeds cloth merchant's house of the early eighteenth century. Its unknown architect based the design of the doorway and large central window on drawings in Domenico de Rossi's book *Studio d'Architettura Civile* published in Rome in 1702. This shows that Leeds was by no means a provincial backwater at this time.

When Austhorpe Hall was built by John More in 1694, it made a remarkable break with the local tradition of stone walls, heavy mullioned windows and robustly carved oak woodwork. Instead, it was built in brick with stone details, light wooden window-frames and all the symmetrical grace and elegance of the coming Georgian era. Inside, the transformation was just as great, its staircase being carved to the highest standards. Regrettably this feature was removed from the house late in the nineteenth century, and rebuilt into Seacroft Grange, where it is seen here.

This fine house, which stood at the corner of South Brook Street and Hunslet Lane, in Hunslet, was probably built early in the eighteenth century by the Brook family. Its elegant pilasters, tall sash windows and long nine-bay façade all provide ample evidence for the lifestyle of Leeds merchants of this period.

Alderman John Brook, Mayor of Leeds in 1736, lived here, succeeding generations of his family providing the town with further mayors in 1754, 1800 and 1814.

Regrettably this building too was a victim of twentieth-century redevelopment, coming down in 1932.

Denison Hall, the finest house erected in Leeds by any of its prosperous merchant families, was built by John Denison in 1786. Constructed with 13,680 cubic yards of stone in the remarkably short time of 101 days, it enjoyed every convenience including a billiard room, a library, a 60ft by 20ft ballroom, fifteen bedrooms, plus servants accommodation, coach houses, stabling for fourteen horses, a brew-house, a wash-house, and finally a richly-planted six acre garden offering delightful views to the south across the verdant Aire Valley. Even so, it is unlikely that its builder actually took up residence here, for he retired from the merchant life in the late 1780s, and lived as a country gentleman in Nottinghamshire up to his death in 1820.

The interior of Denison Hall has some extremely fine architectural features, including this beautiful staircase in the central hall. Dr Kirk, founder of the York Castle Museum, was brought here on 20 February 1940, when the Hall was a private nursing home. In fact, his last words recorded as he was carried up to the first floor, were 'Oh, I'd like that for my museum!'

When Benjamin Gott purchased the manor of Armley in 1804, Armley House was a relatively plain building of around 1781. Between 1801 and 1822 he transformed the appearance of the estate by having it re-designed by Humphrey Repton, the leading landscape architect of the day. He then turned his attention to the house itself, employing Sir Robert Smirke to convert it into this elegant Greek Revival villa, a suitable home both for the Gott family and for their outstanding collections of paintings and sculpture. To ensure their safety, Armley House now incorporated substantial fire-proofing features, such as vaulted masonry floors supported by cast-iron beams, and stone and iron-framed back-stairs. Today this former home of the Gott family serves as a club-house for the Gott's Park golf course.

Thomas Nicholson, a wealthy shipping magnate and stockbroker, purchased the estate we now know as Roundhay Park in 1803 as a country seat for his family. Over the coming years the Nicholsons landscaped the parkland, created the lakes, and built Roundhay church, almshouses and day school. For their own accommodation, they employed John Clark to design the Mansion House around 1826. Behind the Greek Revival façade with its Corinthian portico lay suites of elegant reception rooms and a grand staircase leading up to the first floor. Ever since the Corporation purchased the park in 1872, the mansion has been used as a hotel to provide refreshments for its numerous visitors.

These two carved stone skulls are set into the wall of a former stable in Crown Court, the narrow alley which runs from Kirkgate through to the Corn Exchange. According to local tradition, they commemorate two men who were sleeping in the straw here after being press-ganged into the army, and suffocated during the night.

This photograph is not particularly inspiring, but it does record the view which greeted most visitors as they entered the city centre by the main road from London and the south. Bridge End in the 1890s had already lost most of the fine Georgian mansions which once made it a pleasant, almost rural, suburb sporting large wooded gardens with summer-houses. With the exception of the block in the centre, next to Leeds Bridge, virtually everything here is Victorian, although a number of

earlier merchants houses etc. were to be found down Dock Street to the right.

Some of the more interesting aspects of this photograph are in its minor details — the horse-drawn carts, omnibuses and carrier's cart, the range of advertisements, and, perhaps most surprising of all, the appearance of a shepherd leaning on his crook while casually chatting in the middle of the main road. Today this activity would be instantly fatal!

Despite being Leeds' most important and most prosperous street for almost eight hundred years, Briggate has remained an architectural jumble in terms of the scale and style of its buildings. This is clearly seen in this photograph taken from its junction with Duncan Street around 1900. In the left-hand foreground stands Sutton's fashions, with its Italianate

balustrade of the 1860s, this being followed by a 'Jacobean town house', a Renaissance façade in terracotta, some 'tudor' half-timbering, a genuine Leeds merchant's house, probably of the early eighteenth century, and then a great continental chateau. It is little better today, the modernist additions of the 1960s being particularly intrusive.

In 1865 the North Eastern Railway obtained an act which permitted the building of a new line to link those from the south and west of the country, which had terminated at Wellington Street, with those from the north and east, which came into Marsh Lane Station, at the other side of town. As a result, the new City Station was built, together with a high brick viaduct of 1866-69 which sliced through the centre of Leeds, crossing Briggate by means of this 54ft bridge. In town planning terms it was a disaster, for it permanently separated the town from its waterfront, and further divided it into an industrial area to the south, and a commercial and residential area to the north, a division which is still very evident today.

Despite its great prosperity, the centre of Leeds retained many early buildings along the frontages of its major streets up to comparatively recent times. This is the west side of Lower Briggate in the early 1860s, still with probably sixteenth-century timber-framed buildings of one or two storeys, their façades being of seventeenth-century brick with an accumulation of later shop fronts. From left to right are John Barracloughs, hosier (with his window full of stockings), and William Bolland, printer, both in a fine merchants' house, then James Lowley, bootmaker, and the three shops of the Pickard family, Anthony selling wines and spirits, Julia selling tobacco, and Daniel selling drapery. Beyond, rising above the old houses fronting on to Boar Lane, rises R.D.Chantrell's tower of Holy Trinity Church, erected in 1841.

This photograph, taken in 1900-01, shows how every available inch of Briggate property was being used for commercial purposes. Behind the mass of adverts (few of which would meet today's planning conditions), these three shops housed, left: the Maypole Dairy Company, centre: Bean and Sons, stationers, Rowntree & Co. chocolate makers, Brooks, Pickup, colliery proprietors, William Scriven, estate agent and rent collector, and, right: E.Sillers, furriers.

In addition, the entry led through to the Mercury Old Office Yard, where the town's major newspaper used to be printed.

The Rose and Crown Yard, seen here in 1887, stood on the site of the present Queen's Arcade in Briggate. This typical Leeds yard, with its mixture of stone flagged and set-paved road surface, was occupied by Morley's Temperance Hotel on the left, and Binks' Rose and Crown Hotel on the right, while beyond were Mr Askey's second-hand clothes shop, and a range of joiners and cabinet makers' shops, a coffee roasters, a fishmongers, tobacconists, plumbers and tinners shops.

It was here, in 1831, that James Norton was arrested when trying to place a box containing the body of Robert Hudson, recently removed from East Ardsley churchyard by bodysnatchers, on the coach to Edinburgh.

By the end of the nineteenth century many of the yards built on Leeds' medieval burgage plots off Briggate had degenerated into a very poor state. Here we can see Pack Horse Yard from its Lands Lane entrance, the buildings on the right forming the warehousing, etc. for the shops fronting on to Commercial Street. Note the open gully running down the centre of the yard towards the Pack Horse itself.

Before being cleared in the 1880s Wood Street ran between Vicar Lane and Briggate approximately along the line of the present County Arcade. On the left, halfway down the street, are metalworkers' and barber shops, followed by the Boy and Barrel Hotel, where carriers set off to carry parcels, etc. to Otley, Thorner and Aberford. At the end of the street, above the archway into Briggate, was Parkin's Temperance Hotel and Dining Rooms, while to the right was the Boot and Shoe Inn. The narrow entry at the side of the inn lead into a small square court, Boot and Shoe yard, lined with blind-back cottages. Although not a healthy area, it did not share the notorious reputation of its namesake off Kirkgate.

Up to 1867 the streets of central Leeds still retained their original dimensions. Since they were now far too narrow either to take the ever-increasing volume of road traffic, or to reflect the town's growing prosperity, the Corporation now began a series of major road-widening schemes, commencing with Boar Lane. This photograph shows the entrance to Boar Lane from Briggate just before all the left-hand side was demolishd in order to bring it to its present width. John T.Beer was a clothier, hatter, and poet who adopted the novel advertising method of giving away a volume of his poetical works to anyone who spent over £1 at his shop.

This view of upper Briggate around 1910 shows a number of new developments. To the left, for example, Percy Robinson's buff-coloured terracotta jeweller's shop marks the entrance to Albion Place, while to the right are the recently-completed Leeds Estates Company buildings. As the *Yorkshire Post* commented 'One has only to think of the state of things that existed a few years ago, and glance at the stately building now practically finished, to realise the vastness of the improvement that has

been affected. Ten years ago we had abattoirs in the very heart of the city,' on the site occupied by these buildings.

Today we can still appreciate the brick-red and orange terracotta of these façades, particularly since all the flamboyant Edwardian advertising signs have now disappeared.

After being widened in the 1860s, Boar Lane developed as the most fashionable shopping centre in Leeds, the quality and uniform height of its buildings contrasting greatly with the mongrel assortment lining Briggate. Trevellyan Chambers in the distance adopted the Mansard roofs and Renaissance features of France, while those nearer to the camera employed Yorkshire stone carved in the most elegant styles of Continental Gothic. The whole scene here around 1905 is one of bustle and activity, everyone being encouraged to enjoy the delights of the Grand Restaurant, the White Horse Restaurant, Fairburn's Restaurant, or purchase the wares of the Yorkshire Rubber Company, etc.

Up to the mid nineteenth century Kirkgate had the air of decaying elegance of a fine Georgian country town. Some of the wealthy cloth merchants' houses still lined its pavements, although they were now divided up into multiple residential and commercial occupancy. The rebuilding of the Parish Church in 1838-41, followed by the construction of the railway bridge in 1866-9, destroyed much of this atmosphere however, leaving it as a decidedly second-rate area in comparison to the elegant new streets being constructed in the central areas of the town.

In this photograph we can see just how narrow Vicar Lane was before it was demolished for widening in 1899. On the right, the Crown Hotel stands just north of the covered market, while on the left in the area of today's King Edward Street, are the entrances to Fleet Street and Leadenhall Street. No.11 was George Braithwaite's boot and shoe shop; No.12-13 was A.M.Cowood's provision dealers; No.14 was John Smith's outfitters; No.15, J.F.White's chemists; and No.16 was Owen Genty's Dolphin Inn.

Park Square was developed as an elegant residential area between 1788 and 1810, most of the houses here being constructed by speculative builders for sale to the wealthy merchant and gentry population of Leeds. Delightfully situated at the West End of the town, it benefited from the fresh, clean breezes blowing down the Aire Valley. This advantage was soon lost, however, as the rapid development of massive factories a short distance up-wind began to swathe it in a shroud of dense black smoke. This only disappeared following the adoption of clean-air acts in the 1960s, after which the square regained something of its original character as a delightfully peaceful oasis within the centre of the city.

Commercial Street around 1900, with Lands Lane to the left, and Kirkgate in the distance. Cars have now begun to invade the city's fashionable shopping streets, although there is still room for ladies with hand-carts, or for William Game to take his flat cart of fruit and potatoes down to his stall in Kirkgate Market. Local directories give further details of the shops which once traded

here, the Church Army and the Christian Scientists, above the clothiers on the left, are followed by Kunzle's confectionary, Hopkinson's music shop, the Woods, tailors and dressmakers, and W.H.Smith, while on the right are Field's Oriental Cafe, Williams' costumiers, Wray's restaurant, James Bacon's photographers and finally the Irish Linen Company.

By the Edwardian period, Park Row had already developed as the heart of the city's economic life, as it still remains today. Each building reflected the pride and prosperity of its company, as banks and insurance companies competed to outdo each other in architectural grandeur. In the foreground stands Priestly Hall, named after Dr Joseph Priestly, who was minister at the adjacent

Mill Hill Chapel in the eighteenth century. Built as the chapel's
school by George Corson in 1858-59, it was demolished for new
office development in 1968.

This view, taken from the windows of the former Yorkshire Banking Company at the junction of Boar Lane and Bishopgate Street, was taken around 1889, just before every building seen here was demolished in order to create City Square. Wellington Street leads off to the left, the large central block housing the Midland Hotel, while the next street leads directly into the Coloured Cloth Hall, with its octagonal cupola. Next comes Infirmary Street, and the General Post Office (formerly the courthouse) which faces on to Park Row off to the right. The shadows show that this photograph was taken around mid-day, but still there is hardly a vehicle in sight, and it is still possible to stand around in the road without any real danger.

Here we see City Square around 1930, when, as its promoters envisaged, it formed the major focal point of city life. All the monumental buildings proudly erected by the previous couple of generations stand intact, albeit stained a uniform black by the foul Leeds atmosphere. On the left the pinnacles of Mill Hill Chapel arise behind the Black Prince; then, behind the War Memorial, stands the Royal Exchange by T.H. & F.Healey of 1872. The northern side of Boar Lane has some fine buildings too, the lighter-coloured block being a cast-iron Gothic warehouse of 1873 by Thomas Ambler. Then, beyond the green dome of W.Gwyther's bank of 1899 comes W.B.Perkin's Queen's Hotel of 1863.

This 1942 view of City Square from Bishopgate Street is framed by the Queen's Hotel on the left, and the Midland Bank on the right. The huge white-glazed terracotta building seen across the square was erected as the offices of the Standard Life Assurance Company in 1901 on the site of the former courthouse. Behind its classical façade were fifty suites of offices occupied by stock and insurance brokers, manufacturers, business and manufacturing consultants, transport contractors, and schools of accounting, banking and insurance.

Its replacement by the monolithic Norwich Union building did little to improve the character of Leeds' architecture.

This street of half-timbered shops, complete with their beautifully carved barge-boards and deeply overhanging eaves, looks as if it might be part of Chester. In fact, it was of a similar date to many of the Chester 'Rows', having been built around 1901, on the western side of New Briggate. The only example of this style of architecture to be seen in the City today stands in nearby Merrion Street, for this whole block was demolished in the early 1960s.

To most people living in Leeds today, it is almost inconceivable that the narrow street shown in this photograph of 1928 could actually be the Headrow looking west from Vicar Lane. Virtually the only recognisable building is the terracotta fronted Three Legs Hotel, a few doors down on the left-hand side. Up to this date 'Lowerhead Row' and 'Upperhead Row' were still close to their original size, but then the City Council swept away the whole of the northern side of these streets, including Lloyd's Bank seen here on the right, to create The Headrow, the finest street of truly metropolitan scale in the whole of Yorkshire.

This is the same view taken in July 1931. The small shop and the 'Three Legs' sign can still be seen on the left, the kerb stones of the former Lowerhead Row now appearing below the fencing in the middle of the Headrow. In place of the old Lloyd's Bank, a new one has been built on the new, wider street-line. The uniform façade, designed by Sir Reginald Bloomfield in a solid late seventeenth-century manner reminiscent of Christopher Wren, was intended to run from Quarry Hill to Cookridge Street. Unfortunately it remained unfinished when war broke out, and the blocks erected to complete the scheme in the post-war period certainly lack this high quality.

The major site along the new Headrow was taken by Lewis' department store. Between 1930 and 1938 Messrs Atkinson & Shaw's design for this massive building was gradually brought towards completion at a cost of over £900,000 including the price of the land. This photograph of 1934 shows the lower half of the store. On its opening day, 17 September 1932, 120,000 customers had flooded through its doors, marvelling at its polished marble walls, bronze decorated staircases, its lifts and escalators, all of which added a touch of modern glamour to their shopping expeditions.

The Dark Arches beneath City Station are one of Leeds' most dramatic yet least-known features. They are best appreciated shortly after a heavy rainfall, when the waters of the River Aire thunder beneath this iron bridge with all the drama of a Gustave Doré engraving. A Victorian ballad tells the story of a young man who was enticed down here by a pretty young damsel, whom he entertained with lobster, oysters and brandy, before her burly accomplice appeared, beat him, robbed him, and left him lying naked in the gutter!

'Now all you young chaps take warning by me,
And never go a-courting when you're on the spree,
And never take those ladies out of their way
Down by the dark arches under the railway.'

Today there are no such risks, particularly since the development of Granary Wharf and the craft markets which now take place here every Sunday.

It is probable that the first church in Leeds was built by Paulinus early in the seventh century. There was certainly a church here by the time of the Domesday survey, one which gradually developed into a very large and impressive central-towered structure by the mid-sixteenth century. During the eighteenth and early nineteenth centuries a variety of repairs and improvements were carried out, but a restoration project started in 1838 by the Revd W.F.Hook, the Vicar of Leeds, resulted in the whole church being demolished and rebuilt in its present form.

R.D.Chantrell's design in the Decorated/Perpendicular Gothic style gave Leeds one of the best parish churches of its period, but, even so, we must still wonder if it was really necessary to have demolished its medieval predecessor.

Since the Parish Church of St Peter served an extremely populous area, it was provided with pews both at ground level and in sloping galleries so as to provide some 3,000 sittings. As this photograph shows it is a very large and spacious church, admirably designed for effective preaching from the pulpit. Music for the services comes from the choir, which occupies the stalls just in front of the altar steps, and from the fine organ, seen to the right, in the south transept. Leeds has been fortunate in enjoying some of this country's finest church music over the past 150 years.

St John's Church, New Briggate, is one of Yorkshire's greatest architectural treasures. In 1715, Ralph Thoresby stated that it was 'so noble and stately a Structure as is scarce to be parallel'd in England, as founded, finished and liberally endow'd by one Person, John Harrison, Esq., a Native and chief glory of this populous Town . . .It was consecrated by Archbishop Neile, 21 September 1634, when the Founder was First Alderman of the Corporation.' This late nineteenth-century view shows the graveyard filled with the flat ledger-stones so typical of this region. They marked the graves of many Leeds inhabitants, from inn-keepers to an actor, a Cashmere printer, and even a German prince, Frederick William De Holzendorf, who died in 1771.

The unique interior of St John's Church survived intact through to the late 1860s. By that time its design was at complete variance with the high Victorian view of what a church should be, and proposals were made for its demolition. Fortunately, R.N.Shaw and G.G.Scott, the finest church architects of the day, were able to argue in favour of its preservation. However, the ensuing 'restoration' was a disaster; the walls were stripped, the ornate cresting removed from the screen, the pulpit was cut down, re-sited, and had its sounding board removed, all the pews were rearranged, and the reading-desk disappeared. This photograph of the 1870s shows it in this bleak condition, before the Revd John Scott made good as much of the damage as he possibly could between 1884 and 1898.

Right: In 1722 the leading merchants of Leeds joined with Lady Elizabeth Hastings of Ledson Hall to build a new church on Boar Lane. The architect, William Etty of York, produced both a drawing and a wooden model for the guidance of the workmen when building this elegant Doric structure. The gold fleece which ornamented both the lead fall-pipes, and the weather-vane of the original spire, showed that Holy Trinity was intended to be used exclusively by the wealthy cloth merchants and gentry of the town, a fact confirmed by their purchase of most of the pews.

This unique photograph was taken in the late 1860s when the south side of Boar Lane had been demolished for road-widening. It shows the complete south façade, and the three new upper stages of the tower added in 1839 to the designs of R.D.Chantrell.

The interior of Holy Trinity provided a worthy setting for the worship of the fashionable Leeds merchant class. It probably owes much to the London churches of the period, being essentially a city church. It still retains its original 1723-7 appearance, with the exception of the bases of the pillars, which were lowered by two feet when the present pews were installed in 1887.

The fashionable West End of Georgian Leeds demanded a fashionable church, and so, in 1791-3, St Paul's was built on the south-east corner of Park Square. The architect, William Johnson of Leeds, designed the end walls as Ionic temple fronts, the western gable being surmounted by a tall tower which formed a major local landmark until 1905, when the whole site was cleared. Now the only reminders of the existence of this church are St Paul's Street, a number of souvenirs which incorporate stone, wood and brass from the church, and photographs such as this.

The interior of St Paul's was, in essence, a great open preaching house, the traditional Church of England chancel being reduced to a small apse at the east end. Unlike Holy Trinity, there were no massive stone pillars to support the roof. Instead, there was a single-span roof which enabled most of the 1,175 worshippers to gain an uninterrupted view of the altar and the preacher in the pulpit. Note the galleries and their elegant supports.

The church of St John, Adel, is the most complete Norman church in the county, being erected around 1140 in the form of a simple nave and chancel, separated by a richly-carved chancel arch. Over the succeeding centuries it lost its original roof and belfry, and gained a number of new windows, but a series of restorations mainly by Chantrell in 1838 and Street in 1878 corrected most of these faults, while wisely allowing the large late medieval windows to continue to light the nave. The corbel frieze of human and animal faces around the eaves, and the carvings of Christ in Majesty and the symbols of the evangelists over the south doorway, together with its great bronze closing-ring, are all worthy of detailed study.

The church of St George, Great George Street, was built to the designs of John Clark in 1836-8 to meet the demands of the town's increasing population. Its two outstanding features were its 160ft spire, which blew down in the great gale of 1962, an its extensive vaults. These were originally intended for intramural burials, but all internments here stopped in 1855. In 1930, in the depths of the Depression, the Revd Don Robins used this space to found St George's Crypt as a hostel for homeless men, offering bread, soup, and beds on hard benches. This work continues to be needed as much as ever, and so the Crypt has expanded the range of its services to meet the demands of today's society.

The first St Bartholomew's Church at Armley was built in 1630, the second in 1834-5, and the third and present church in 1872 to the designs of Messrs Walker and Athron, architects, of East Parade. Built in the Early English style in local gritstone, its bold outline dominates most views of south Leeds. In this photograph, it is very evident that the stone of the church itself had already become blackened by the infamous Leeds soot-laden atmosphere by the time the 153ft high tower was added. Since that time the whole church has assumed the same tone, regrettably hiding the fine details seen here. Note the rope-lashed scaffolding still in position at roof level.

The chapel of St Mary the Virgin was the major place of worship in the populous South Leeds township of Hunslet. This photograph, taken around 1860, shows the original brick chapel built in 1636 and enlarged in 1744, and the elegant Grecian tower added in 1832-3. In 1862 the whole of this building was demolished to make way for a new Gothic-revival church designed by Perkins & Backhouse of Leeds.

The area just behind the church was the traditional site of Hunslet Feast, an annual celebration attended by a wide range of sideshows and entertainments.

As the Harehills area began to develop in the 1880s, a new parish was established there to meet the demands of the rapidly expanding population. Between 1891 and 1904 the new church of St Aidan gradually rose above the close-packed terrace housing. In contrast to the traditional Gothic churches in other parts of Leeds, the architect R.J.Johnson drew his inspiration from the great Romanesque basilicas of early medieval Italy to produce this magnificent church. R.H.Kitson, one of the parishoners, commissioned Frank Brangwyn, one of the finest of all British artists, to paint the curved wall of the apse with scenes from the life of St Aidan. Instead, Brangwyn suggested using mosaic, since it would not be discoloured by the foul Leeds atmosphere. As a result, the vast mosaic seen here was completed between 1913 and 1916. Without doubt, St Aidan's is one of the finest city churches of its period, although it is a great pity that its intended tower was never brought to completion.

These houses in the corner of St Peter's Square, just beyond the Falstaff Inn, were once a cholera and fever hospital, then a school for orphans, with a Parish Church Sunday School on Sundays, then a National Day School, and a Parish Church Mission. By 1870 this was one of the worst slum areas of Leeds, the nearby 'Muck Yard' being a foul, evil-smelling refuse tip. The occupants of this area could not help being infested with vermin and infected with typhoid every summer. In 1881, the Revd John Gott, Vicar of Leeds, pulled these buildings down and replaced them with a new Mission Chapel and Schools of the Good Shepherd, which opened at Whitsuntide, 1882.

The first Mill Hill Chapel was built in 1672 as a Presbyterian meeting house, but by the 1840s its influential Unitarian congregation wanted a chapel rather more 'creditable to their taste'. Having held a competition they chose a design by Bowman and Crowther which incorporated a chancel, transepts, and a wealth of Gothic details which made it look far more like an Anglican church than any of the relatively plain non-conformist churches of the period. Since its opening on 22 December 1848, the chapel has formed a prominent feature of Park Row, and of City Square. One of the Chapel's most significant ministers was Dr Joseph Priestly, scientist, philospher, and discoverer of oxygen, whose statue stands in the square opposite.

The Wesley Chapel, Meadow Lane, was built in 1816 to provide seating for 1,100 worshippers, and was later extended by the addition of the schools to the right. The chapel's posters announce the Revd N.W. Thomlinson's forthcoming sermon on 'Wanted, Recruits', but others may have been tempted to go to the Grand Theatre's production of *The Gay Grisette*. To the left, a lady waits for customers outside her cloth and clothing shop.

Once described as 'one of the largest and most magnificent ecclesiastical buildings in the empire', the Brunswick Methodist Chapel certainly was large and impressive. Erected to the designs of Joseph Botham in 1824-5, it seated a congregation of around 2,500 in box pews and an enormous gallery which swept around the interior. In 1827 it was decided that a vast organ should be installed, to confirm the chapel's pre-eminence in Leeds. Part of the congregation rebelled at the prospect of having an instrument which would please the ear, captivate the passions, and subvert the spirituality of their worship. After a stormy meeting, they founded the Protestant Methodists, and removed elsewhere. In 1984, after all the conservation agencies had tried to find alternative uses, the chapel was regrettably demolished and the site cleared.

This magnificent Doric portico formed the entrance to East Parade Congregational Chapel. This huge building, designed by Moffat and Hurst of Doncaster, commenced with the laying of the foundation stone by Edward Baines in September 1839, and was opened for worship in January 1841. It seated 1,600 people, had a fine organ, and could accommodate 500 pupils in its Sunday Schools. An early victim of the commercial development of this area, it was demolished in 1899, just after this photograph was taken, to make way for the North British and Mercantile Assurance Company. The crowd on the pavement are studying the portraits of VCs 'Soldiers of the Queen, Only a Poor Artist's work to earn a copper of patronage'.

The interior of East Parade Chapel was dominated by this fine organ, which cost some £1,200. In common with the exterior, it takes its design from classical Greece, the use of Corinthian capitals adding to its richness of design. From the reading desk below, the preacher could command the attention of the entire congregation during the course of the services.

In 1836 a property known as Park Terrace on the junction of Cookridge Street and Guildford Street (now the Headrow) was purchased by the Catholic Church for the purpose of building its first major church in the town centre. The Georgian house seen here was already in existence, but now it was used as a presbytery for the priests serving St Anne's. Over the succeeding years, Catholic schools were built on the remainder of the site, but every building was swept away in preparation for the city's road-widening scheme in 1901-04.

It is possible that Mass had been said in Leeds ever since the Reformation, but it was not until 1786-7 that the presence of the Roman Catholic Church was re-established here in the form of the Leeds Mission. The first new chapel was built in Lady Lane in 1793-4, followed by another in York Road in 1831, but as the Catholic population of the town rapidly expanded, it proved possible to replace the Lady Lane Chapel with this fine church of St Anne. Built at the junction of Guildford Street and Cookridge Street in 1837-8 to the designs of John Child, it soon acquired additional status as the Cathedral Church of St Anne on the formation of the Leeds Diocese in 1878.

The new St Anne's Cathedral was built to the designs of J.H.Eastwood between 1902 and 1904, being dedicated on 16 June of that year, just as the old Cathedral began to be demolished. The site was quite restricted, but the architect created a successful if unconventionally planned building in the fashionable Arts and Crafts Gothic style. The use of strong parallel vertical motifs topped by squat finials achieves a remarkable sense of upward thrust in the cathedral, almost as if the finials were holding the whole structure down to earth.

This is the high altar of St Anne's, as it appeared when recently completed around 1904. The carved pine reredos rising behind it was designed by S.K. Greenslade and executed by Flint Brothers of Clapham, London. Its eight niches are filled with statues of saints associated either with the Cathedral or with the history of the Church in Yorkshire. They surround a beautiful carved painted and gilt panel depicting the Coronation of the Virgin. The ornate *baldacchino* or canopy over the altar shows grapes, peppers, pineapples, pomegranates and poppies, all symbols of the Resurrection.

The first synagogue in Leeds opened in 1846, but by 1900, as a result of extensive immigration following the Russian pogroms of 1881, there were about a dozen in operation, the largest being the Belgrave Street Synagogue of 1860-61. In 1927, Stanley Wright & Clay of Albion Street designed the Louis Street Synagogue on Chapeltown Road. It was among the finest buildings to be erected in the city during the inter-war years, its copper-domed brick exterior, enhanced by a stone portico, etc. being handsome enough, but still leaving the visitor quite unprepared for the scale and quality of the great domed synagogue within. This photograph shows the Ark, framed in its great slabs of beautifully veined marble.

As the Jewish community gradually moved out of the central area of the city around North Street up into the more northerly suburbs, new synagogues had to be established. The New Vilna Synagogue on Harrogate Road, Moortown, was opened on 6 September 1959. Its stylish 1930s design by James Brodie of Pudsey came from its original use as the Kingsway Cinema, which had opened on 28 June 1937.

In the early nineteenth century the over-crowded mass of burials both inside churches and in inner-city churchyards was a cause of great concern throughout the whole country. In Leeds, as in other large towns, one solution was the establishment of private burial grounds in pleasant suburban surroundings. The Leeds General Cemetery Company purchased St George's Fields in Woodhouse in 1833, and then, after setting up an architectural competition, used John Clark's designs to erect a high perimeter wall, a massive and sombre gatehouse lodge, and this Greek Ionic temple. Although it looks as if it should be a cemetery chapel, it was never consecrated, for at this period there were considerable differences between the town's various religious groups.

In 1756-8 the Coloured or Mixed Cloth Hall was erected by public subscription to house the Tuesday and Saturday markets in unfinished cloth woven from dyed wool. It was a vast U-shaped building measuring 381ft by 198ft, occupying virtually the whole area of the present City Square and Post Office. As contemporary writers commented, it exceeded any building of its kind in Europe. The pedimented entrance wing closing the end of the courtyard, together with the octagonal domed building in the foreground, were added around 1780 to provide further space where the merchants and the trustees of the hall could conduct their business.

The Corporation purchased the hall for £66,000 in 1889 so that its site could be cleared for their new scheme of civic improvements.

Nos 99-100 Kirkgate look like a simple block of early nineteenth-century shops, but, as historians have always known, and as local planners 'discovered' in the 1980s, they form part of the original White Cloth Hall of 1711. When first built, the two wings, indicated by the hipped roofs, enclosed a deep courtyard lined by an open arcade at ground level, and topped by a gilded cupola. Here clothiers from parishes to the south and west of Leeds stored their cloth ready for inspection by the merchants every Tuesday afternoon. The success of this venture was so great that it confirmed Leeds as the greatest cloth market in Britain and ensured the town's growing prosperity over the following centuries.

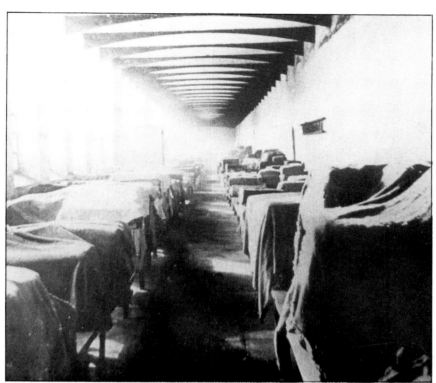

The interior of the Coloured Cloth Hall was laid out in 'streets', this being the traditional way in which cloth had been displayed for sale on the earlier open-air stalls set out in Lower Briggate on market days. They were variously known as 'Cheapside', 'Queen Street', 'Mary's Lane', 'Change Alley' and 'King Street'. Here the hand-loom weavers or clothiers displayed their cloth on one of the 1,800 stalls so that it could be inspected and purchased by a merchant who would then complete the finishing processes and arrange for its sale throughout every part of the known world.

Leeds' third White Cloth Hall was built in 1775 on a plot of tenter-close purchased from the trustees of Leeds Grammar School. Its four wings enclosed the whole of a vast irregular quadrangle measuring some 300 by 210 feet, extending from the houses on Kirkgate down to the Calls. Both the clock and its elegant stone cupola were removed here from the second White Cloth Hall when that building was demolished in 1786. As at the Coloured Cloth Hall, its interior was divided into streets, here containing 1,213 stalls where the weavers could display their undyed and unfinished woollen cloth for sale on market days. In the 1860s the hall was sliced in two by the North Eastern Railway viaduct, so that trading had to be transferred to a fourth White Cloth Hall on King Street. Afterwards this entrance block served a variety of industrial purposes, before being beautifully restored by Speciality Shops in 1991.

The prosperous merchant class of Georgian Leeds required a suite of high-quality rooms to house all their fashionable balls, concerts, and other festivities. To do this, they decided to build a very grand upper-storey above the northern wing of their White Cloth Hall, incorporating card-rooms, supper-rooms, and a magnificent ballroom with free-standing Corinthian columns supporting a highly ornate covered plaster ceiling. It was opened on 9 June 1777, 'with a minuet by Lady Effingham and Sir George Saville, when upwards of two hundred and twenty of the nobility and gentry were present; the appearance of the ladies and gentlemen was more brilliant than ever remembered.'

From the 1860s it served as a warehouse, first for fireplaces, and then for tobacco, but now it is about to be restored to its original grandeur.

When the courthouse was first built at the bottom end of Park Row, it provided the town with a fine courtroom which could accommodate 800 people both for the courts and for a variety of public meetings. Thomas Taylor's original design of 1813 had the large portico flanked by single-storey wings incorporating Coade Stone panels showing the Golden Fleece of Leeds and the crossed fasces as carried before Roman justices. In 1834 it was enlarged by the addition of a first floor designed by R.D.Chantrell, but then lost its original use after the courts were transferred to the new Town Hall. After serving as the main post office in Leeds for forty years and having a second floor added in 1872 to house GPO telegraph equipment, it was finally demolished in 1901.

The Leeds Cavalry Barracks occupied the area between Roundhay Road and Chapeltown Road just to the north of the city centre, the present Barrack Road running through the area of their parade ground. The barracks themselves, long ranges of brick-built stables, cavalrymen's accommodation, etc. were erected along the high, south-facing ridge along the northern edge of the site in 1820 at a cost of £28,000. Throughout its active life there was usually the best part of a regiment of cavalry or artillery stationed here, this photograph showing 'M' battery of the Royal Horse Artillery commanded by Major R.W.Breeks posing here in May 1913.

In the 1960s and '70s the barracks were used for a variety of commercial purposes, up to demolition in 1988-9. Some of the railings from the gallery still survive, however, being rescued for re-use in a similar situation at Armley Mills, the city's industrial museum.

The Leeds Rifles, the 7th West Yorkshire Rifle Volunteers, were formed in 1859. After a number of fund-raising events, including a bazaar in the Town Hall and a dramatic entertainment in the Royal Amphitheatre in 1862, they were able to build this armoury and drill ground at 27 Oxford Place. It opened on 2 May 1863 with an inspection of the corps by Lt Colonel Harman, the occasion probably being commemorated by this photograph.

Leeds is renowned as a great Victorian city, but this was only achieved by the sacrifice of a number of fine Georgian buildings, such as John Clark's Ionic Commerical Buildings at the junction of Boar Lane and City Square. Lepton Dobson laid the foundation stone on 18 May 1826, and it opened three years later. Some idea of its size may be obtained by the columns, each of which was 40ft high and 4ft in diameter. Regretably it was swept away in 1871 to provide space for the spiky Gothic horrors of the West Bar building, which was demolished almost a century later for a building of even worse quality.

The interiors of the Commercial Buildings were of great magnificence, the vestibule leading into a grand staircase hall, a room 34ft in diameter rising 60ft to an ornamental dome, supported on twenty Corinthian columns. To the right-hand side extended this news or reading room, 65ft long, 33ft high, and 25ft wide. Here, for an annual subscription of 25s (£1.25) members could come and read all the most useful newspapers and magazines of the day.

For centuries, the corn merchants attending Leeds market had stood in the area called Cross Parish near the market cross at the top of Briggate. When the block of buildings occupying the centre of this space were cleared away in 1825, plans were made to build a new Corn Exchange at the junction of Upper and Lower Headrow. The foundation stone was laid on 31 May 1826 by Mr John Cawood, the whole building, designed by Mr S.Chapman of Leeds, being opened for trade in 1829. In this photograph, taken before its demolition in 1868, we can see the clock and the statue of Queen Anne which had been re-sited here from the former Moot Hall.

A piazza included in the exchange was occupied by the dealers from 11am to 1pm every Tuesday, the remainder of the space being used as offices, auction rooms and an inn.

The Corn Exchange is one of Britain's finest mid-Victorian buildings. Realising that the old Corn Exchange was far too small for the expanding trade, the Markets Committee of the Corporation set up a competition for the design of a much larger structure to be built on an awkwardly-shaped plot on Call Lane. It was won by Cuthbert Brodrick, who conceived a unique oval plan, with two storeys of offices surrounding a central hall. Even in its soot-blackened condition, as seen here, the bold diamond-pointed rustication of its masonry gave constant interest to the play of light across its exterior. Completed in 1862, it continues to fulfil its original function to the present day.

The exterior of the Corn Exchange is bold and dramatic in its design, but even this hardly prepares the visitor for the scale and majesty of the interior. Around the walls are two tiers of arches in coloured and moulded brickwork, each giving access to a particular corn-factor's office, the upper tier being served by a broad gallery edged with cast-iron railings. Above rises the great elliptical dome, 75ft to its highest point, and a masterpiece of Victorian engineering. The large glazed panels were designed to provide the optimum quality of natural lighting on to the floor below, so that those trading at the small black desks could accurately judge the quality of the merchandise.

Although the Corn Exchange still operates in this room, it has recently been sympathetically converted into a modern high-quality shopping and cafe area, where shoppers, visitors and office workers can all enjoy its unique atmosphere.

Within a few years of its completion, the stonework of Leeds Town Hall had been deeply stained to a uniform dense black. This tended to enhance, rather than subdue, its sense of self-assured majesty. Most local people quite forgot that it had once been a warm cream colour, and actually believed that contractors were painting it white when it began to be cleaned in 1971-72. This photograph of around 1902 shows the Town Hall with its lions carved by W.D.Keyworth and added in 1867. A popular local tradition states that they will get up and walk around the building when they hear the clock strike twelve — a feat that no one has yet observed — since they are all stone deaf!

Opposite page, lower: Whenever television news programmes feature local government, a picture of Leeds Town Hall always fills the screen, for, ever since it was built, it has been *the* potent symbol of local democracy. It has not a single trace of hesitation in its design, being superlatively dominant and self-confident. This is a considerable tribute to both the architect and those City Fathers who actually pulled the scheme through, for its creation was characterised by indecision, dithering, and the bankruptcy of its first contractor.

The competition for the design of the Town Hall had been won in open contest by Cuthbert Brodrick, a very young and relatively untried architect from Hull, his scheme being based on four great corner pavilions joined by huge Corinthian colonnades, with the majestic tower rising above the main south-facing frontage. Here we see it in 1858, just before Queen Victoria came to perform the opening ceremony. The freshly-quarried West Yorkshire stone still maintains its pale buff colour, while the timber scaffolding has just been erected for the construction of the great lead-covered dome.

The first-floor rooms along the east side of the Town Hall provided an impressive reception suite for the Mayor. The richly-patterned wallpaper and carpet, the deeply-buttoned Chesterfield settee, and the giltwood chairs used when Queen Victoria opened the building in 1858, all give a very luxurious atmosphere, particularly when illuminated by the crystal chandeliers. This photograph was taken on 26 July 1888 on the occasion of a visit by the Shah of Persia.

As built, the Victoria Hall in Leeds Town Hall was truly magnificent, but gradually its quality began to be eroded, the crystal chandeliers disappearing in 1893, for example, while early in the present century all the gilding, marbling and stencilling was obliterated beneath insipid pastel shades of paintwork. Similarly the great organ was allowed to decay, no major overhaul being carried out between 1904 and 1960. Fortunately the increasing appreciation of Victorian architecture in the 1970s saw the full restoration of the original scheme of decoration, and of the organ, to their true glory.

Standing at the opposite side of Calverley Street to the Town Hall, the Municipal Buildings are one of Leeds' most underrated examples of Victorian architecture. Designed by George Corson, they were opened in 1884 to provide accommodation for the borough's administrative staff. To ensure its security, the central door is guarded by an iron portcullis which is still wound up from beneath the stairs every evening. Inside the entrance hall, an ornate roundel shows a burgher of medieval Leeds paying his bag of money to the treasurer, who records the payment with a quill pen in a large rate book, while the mayor presides over all.

By the 1920s, the office accommodation in the Town Hall and Municipal Buildings was proving totally inadequate for the needs of twentieth-century Leeds, and so the city decided to erect a new civic headquarters incorporating the Lord Mayor's Office, the City Council Chamber, and the main administrative departments. The architect, E. Vincent Harris, then completed designs for an interesting pentagonal building, one side being open to a central courtyard, while another provided a grand porticoed entrance front facing down formal gardens towards the Town hall. Ninety per cent of the workforce used in its construction was taken off the local unemployment register, providing welcome work during this period of deep depression. Within three years, all was finished, and the Civic Hall was opened by King George V and Queen Mary on 23 August 1933.

This view shows the entrance front, with its twin 170ft towers topped by gilt bronze owls modelled by the sculptor John Hodge.

The Council Chamber in the Civic Hall provides an impressive setting for the meetings of the full City Council. The Lord Mayor presides from his chair beneath the high canopy of state bearing the city arms, while the councillors occupy three tiers of seats arranged as a large oval, and members of the public sit in galleries at each end of the chamber. All the woodwork is of polished walnut, the frieze being enriched with armorial roundels, while the panelling below is inscribed with the names of every civic leader from Sir John Savile in 1626 through to the present day, along with those of its most distinguished citizens, such as Joseph Priestley, John Smeaton and Matthew Murray.

The South Market extended from Hunslet Lane to Meadow Lane just a short distance south of Leeds Bridge. R.D.Chantrell designed this scheme in 1823 for a company of local shareholders. As its centre, a large circular 'cross' or colonnade for the sale of butter, eggs and poultry stood in the centre of a semi-circular courtyard and further blocks of buildings which, in total, provided accommodation for forty-nine shops, a slaughter house, and eighteen dwellings. In spite of the excellence of its design, its site was never really popular, and it only began to prosper after it became the home of the quarterly Leeds Leather Market.

The first major indoor market building in the centre of Leeds was built at the junction of Duncan Street and New Market Street in 1824-7. Inside, F.Goodwin's design provided fifty-six stalls for fruit, vegetables and dairy produce, with a bazaar for fancy goods around the first floor, while around the outside, at street level, were sixty-seven further shops for butchers and fishmongers. A contemporary description of the Central Market, as 'one of the principal ornaments of the town', was quite accurate. Its quality is still obvious in this photograph taken on 21 June 1895, just after it had been gutted by fire.

The old market and cattle-market site at the junction of Vicar Lane and Kirkgate was redeveloped by the Corporation in 1857, when this market hall was built in cast iron and glass by C.Tilney, with advice from Sir Joseph Paxton of Crystal Palace fame. It provided space for forty-four shops around the outside and thirty-five inside, these opening from 7am in summer, 8am in winter, through to 9pm weekdays, Saturdays till 11pm. When it first opened, local people were impressed by its beautiful 'crystal' appearance when illuminated at night by 200 gas jets. By 1902, however, it had outlived its working life, and was demolished to make way for its magnificent Edwardian successor.

The City Markets in the 1890s. On the left is the eastern side of the cast-iron market hall of 1857, while to the right are the ends of a grid-pattern of two-storey market buildings, five blocks long by three wide, erected in 1875. They remained in use up to 13 December 1975 when they were largely destroyed by an extensive fire (although four of the western blocks still survive today). The present large modern area of the market hall was then built to take their place.

The new City Markets erected to replace the former Kirkgate Markets in 1903-4 are probably the finest market buildings in Britain. The architects, Leeming and Leeming of Halifax, effectively combined predominantly Flemish façades with Venetian domes and art-nouveau detailing to produce this extremely rich and imposing frontage to Vicar Lane. The adjacent Kirkgate front was originally intended to house an hotel, with a spacious restaurant, a billiard room, a coffee room, and a club and tea room, but this never appears to have come into fruition.

This enormous hall, 243ft long by 102ft wide, formed the centre of the new City markets. Within its Burmantofts glazed-brick walls, twenty-four clustered Corinthian columns support the iron-framed glass roof, each spandrel bearing the City's coat of arms in full colour. Below all the shop units have a cast-iron frame with Corinthian columns, thus producing one of the most practical and elegant of market halls. Regrettably the tall clock, which formed such a potent architectural centre-piece to the whole scheme, fell foul of later views of taste, and was removed in 1912 to an open-air site at Oakwood, where it still remains.

Between 1897 and 1901 this huge extension was built on the eastern end of the block shops of the city markets, which can be seen in the background to the left. It was largely occupied by fruit, vegetable, and nurserymen's stalls, where it was possible to buy anything from a melon to an aspidistra. As the country's largest market, it still enjoys an excellent reputation for quality and value, attracting shoppers from a wide area.

To replace the former insanitary slaughter houses and shambles, the City Council erected this fine Wholesale Meat Market in New York Street to the designs of Walter Hanstock & Son of Leeds and Batley. Opened on 24 July 1899, it provided a spacious market hall, slaughter houses, cold stores, chill rooms and offices, a complete system of overhead rails being installed to enable the carcases to be quickly and efficiently moved from one department to another. As with a number of other civic buildings, it incorporated a clock-tower similar to that on Leeds Town Hall.

Animals for the meat trade were traditionally killed and butchered on the east side of upper Briggate, but new slaughterhouses were built in the yards between Briggate and Vicar Lane in the 1820s. This photograph shows Jos Watson's Ledenhall yards in the 1880s. Here animals driven in from Vicar Lane were kept in pounds or 'pininghouses' at cellar or gallery level ready for slaughter. As a report to the borough council stated in 1880, the ventilation was bad, the walls and floors were impossible to clean, drainage was totally inadequate and, particularly on Wednesdays and Thursdays, the principal killing days, the butchers, live and dead animals, meat and offal, were all crowded together on floors steaming and streaming with blood, all of which could be seen by passers-by on the main streets.

After the demolition of the Coloured Cloth Hall and the creation of City Square, this site was allocated for the building of a new General Post Office. Adopting a Renaissance style appropriate to the concept of City Square, the Board of Works' architect, Henry Tanner, created one of Leeds' most imposing public buildings. It was opened in April 1896, this photograph being taken shortly afterwards, while it still retained its pristine freshness.

In 1861, the Leeds Working Men's Institute was established to provide this large section of society with access to a library, a news-room supplied with daily papers and magazines, rooms where draughts or chess could be played, and a wash room provided with water, soap and towels, all for the single payment of one penny per week. The 1867 Working Men's Hall in Park Street offered these facilities from 8.30am to 10.30pm daily. After it had fallen out of use it was granted to St George's Crypt by the Charity Commissioners, but was then demolished in 1987 for the construction of the New Magistrates Courts.

The Leeds Mechanics' Institute was founded in 1824 to provide a library, lectures and practical instruction to mechanics and others. Having amalgamated with the Leeds Literary Institute in 1842, it was soon able to move into premises in South Parade. As membership grew and influential supporters were acquired, it became possible to discuss the erection of a much grander Institute, the result being the Leeds Institute of 1860-65. The three storeys of classrooms and exhibition galleries arranged around a central circular lecture hall could have appeared just like a bulky warehouse, but with Cuthert Brodrick as architect, it emerged as a great palace, the battered and rusticated basement supporting what appears to be a suite of palatial apartments, since the top-lit rooms above are masked by the massive cornice.

The free Grammar School at Leeds was founded in 1552 under the terms of the will of Sir William Sheffield. Since its first buildings were inconvenient, John Harrison, the great Leeds benefactor, provided this new schoolroom entirely at his own cost in 1664. It stood on North Street, not far from his St John's church. Although enlarged in 1692 and 1822, its site had become very congested by 1859, when it moved to new premises on Woodhouse Moor. These buildings were then sold off to Samuel Denison & Sons, who used it as a foundry until demolition in 1898.

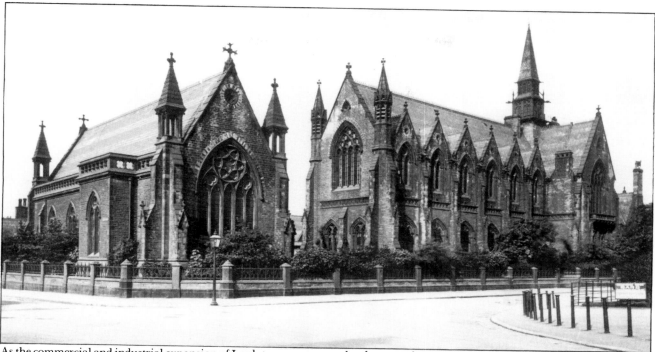

As the commercial and industrial expansion of Leeds town centre engulfed the old grammar school buildings in North Street, it was decided that a new school should be built on a healthier elevated site on the edge of Woodhouse Moor. Work began in 1858, blocks of Potternewton and Weetwood stone being used to construct this fine Geometric Decorated Gothic block of schoolroom, classrooms, gymnasium and changing rooms designed by E.M.Barry.

The chapel was added in 1863 at a cost of £3,000, further additions being made since that time to provide laboratories, a swimming pool, workshops, an art room and more classrooms, so that it could accommodate its increasing number of pupils.

Art education in Leeds first emerged in recognisable form in 1846 when a Government School of Design was established around the classes organised by the Leeds Mechanics' Institute in South Parade. In 1868 the school transferred into the Leeds Institute Building, now the Civic Theatre, where it remained until a new School of Art was built in Vernon Street in 1903.

By today's standards, the teaching was very formal, students progressing from the copying of outlines, through copying shaded drawings, and eventually to making their own drawings from casts of antique sculpture, many of which can be seen around the walls of this studio.

Anatomical demonstrations on the bodies of executed criminals took place at the General Infirmary from 1773, but it was not until 1831 that the Leeds School of Medicine became established in one wing of the Dispensary in North Street. As the School developed, it moved firstly into larger premises in East Parade in 1834, and then into this purpose-built school in Park Street in 1865. It was designed by George Corson, and included a museum, an excellent suite of laboratories, disection rooms, library, council room, and a large lecture theatre with rising semi-circular tiers of bench seats. In 1884 the School became part of the university, and twenty years later moved into new premises in Thoresby Place. After being used by Thackerays, Surgical Instrument Makers, for many years, this building was only recently demolished to make way for a new courthouse.

Since the old premises in Park Street were rapidly proving totally inadequate for the needs of the School of Medicine, a new site was acquired on Thoresby Place, just to the west of the Infirmary. W.H.Thorpe then prepared designs in Tudor Gothic brick and stone, the completed building being opened by the Duke and Duchess of York in October 1894. Today the public can still enjoy the exterior façades of the school, unchanged since this photograph was taken in 1929, but few have any knowledge of the beautiful library and Burmantofts-tiled entrance hall inside.

The leading members of Victorian Leeds' industrial and professional families realised that the highest quality of technical education must be available if the town's prosperity was to continue. They therefore pressed for the establishment of a university here. The Yorkshire College, founded in 1874, became part of the federal Victoria University in 1887, and finally achieved full independence as Leeds University in 1904. The first generation of buildings were designed by Alfred Waterhouse in the typical 'red-brick' Gothic style used by other universities of this period, the Clothworkers Building of 1877 being followed by the Baines Wing of 1882-4, seen here, and the Great Hall of 1891-4.

By the 1920s it had become apparent that the growing importance of Leeds University, and its increasing number of students, now demanded the construction of a large and impressive suite of new buildings. Lanchester and Lodge's scheme extended from the earlier red-brick wings through to the frontage of Woodhouse Lane. Here a broad flight of steps, a portico of great Ionic columns and a high clock-tower stood at the centre of a long façade of gleaming white Portland stone. Due to the war, progress was slow, and it was not until 1950 that the Parkinson Building, seen here, gave the University the prestigious image it required. The great white tower still dominates distant views of the city, even when seen from the Ilkley moors, fourteen miles away.

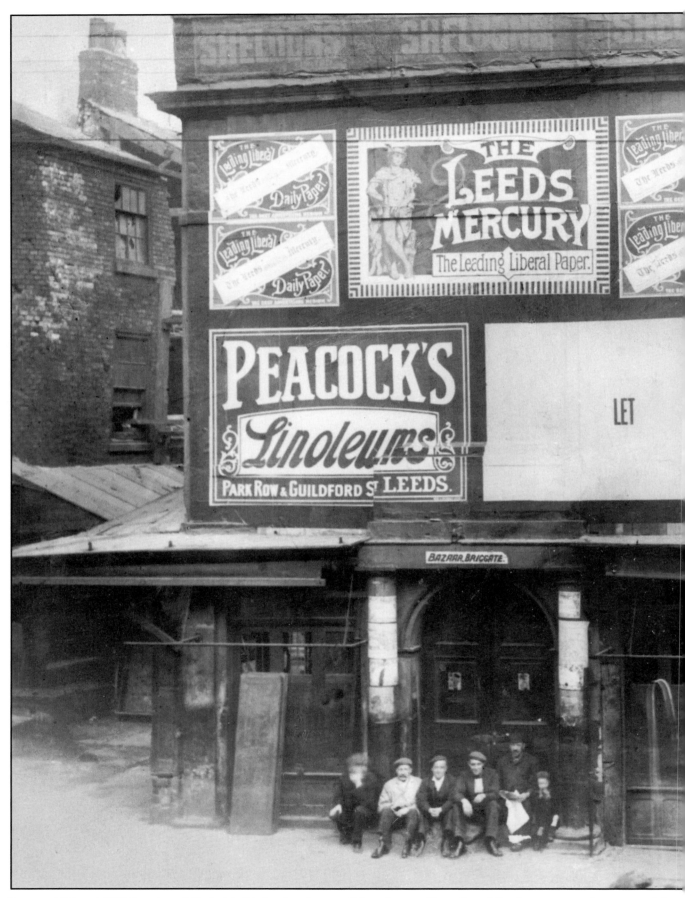

Between 1814 and 1823 Joseph and Frederick Rinder, butchers and cattle dealers, bought up the property between Vicar Lane and Briggate where the County Arcade now stands. They then developed the eastern end of the site with slaughter-houses, meat, fish and vegetable stalls, while the western end was occupied by this building. The Bazaar, which opened in 1826, faced on to Briggate, the ground level shops ranged down both its 219ft sides being used by butchers — their chopping blocks and scales

can be seen lining the open gutter of Cheapside, to the right. Directly beneath the lion modelled under the direction of Joseph Rhodes, the Leeds painter, the double doors gave access to a flight of stairs leading to the first-floor bazaar, where a large range of fancy goods and haberdashery was exhibited for sale in a similar manner to that in today's antique markets. The site was cleared for redevelopment around 1900.

Edward Allen Brotherton, (1856-1930) 1st Baron Brotherton of Wakefield, was the founder of a major chemical empire with factories in Wakefield, Birmingham, Glasgow and Leeds. Through the course of his life he amassed a considerable fortune, and an important library which included many fine manuscripts and early printed books. In 1927 he gave £100,000 for the building of a new Leeds University Library, and was able to lay its foundation stone just before his death. Over the following years his 160ft diameter domed reading-room resting on Swedish green marble pillars rose to completion as the centre of the Brotherton Library, which now holds his personal collection, together with further magnificent collections of books and manuscripts. It was opened by the Archibishop of Canterbury on 6 October 1936.

William Green & Sons, late Buck and Jackson, occupied the last bow-windowed shop in Briggate. The huge grocer's sign takes the form of a giant tea-canister, from which are suspended three golden sugar-cones, the small sign between the windows to the right, meanwhile, shows that the premises were protected by the Norwich Union insurance company. This shop was demolished in 1922, but the entry to the right still gives access to Turk's Head Yard.

Up to 1890 this block of early nineteenth-century shops, including Ross & Co's paint, colour and varnish store with its fine bow windows, and J.W.Foster's fancy drapery, still stood on the west side of Upper Briggate. After being demolished, together with the old Rose and Crown Yard, the site was redeveloped as the present Queen's Arcade.

It is clear that there were no restrictions on tobacco advertising in Edwardian Leeds. Every surface of C.S.Tetley's shop at the junction of Lowerhead Row (The Headrow) and Vicar Lane was covered with a mass of colourful signwriting to promote the various brands of tobacco and cigarettes. Next door stands the former Malt Shovel Inn.

In 1878 the house of Ralph Thoresby, the great Leeds historian, was demolished and replaced by the shops seen here, Nos 16-18 Kirkgate. Jacksons were the 'Cheapest House in the Trade' when buying boots, Fourness and Sons, established in 1828, combined the occupations of chemist and lamp and oil merchants, while Lipton's provided good quality teas, coffees, groceries and bacon, some of the flitches hanging from their fine Gothic Revival frontage. Note the sign of Mr Topliss — Undertaker and Refrigerator Maker!

This block of shops stood at the eastern end of Wellington Street until they were cleared away to create City Square around 1900. In the foreground stands Mrs Elizabeth Cumber's Express Refreshment Rooms, while beyond are three temperance hotels, all conveniently placed to receive travellers arriving at the Central, Wellington and New stations.

For only a few years in the mid 1890s, William Green operated this newsagent and tobacconist's business on the corner of Wade Lane and Lydgate, in the area of the present Merrion Centre. As this 1894 photograph shows, he stocked a wide range of goods, everything from the *Sporting Chronicle's* handicap book to fireworks and even 'Working Class Pills'!

In the 1890s the Leeds Estates Company acquired a large area of narrow yards and streets running between Briggate and Vicar Lane. The entire plot was then cleared and two new streets, Queen Victoria Street and King Edward Street, were created, as well as County and Cross arcades. The architect Frank Matcham was responsible for the whole scheme of 122 shops, the King Edward Hotel, the County Cafe, and its great centre-piece, the Empire Theatre. In this photograph of around 1900-1901, we can see

the completed northern end of the development, while to the south, the final buildings are being demolished to make way for King Edward Street.

Note the Hansom cabs and Broughams standing for hire down the centre of Briggate, and the elegant lamp standards which then lit the city's major streets. The street on the left was first called 'New Bond Street' but this was shortly to be changed to the 'Queen Victoria Street' we know today.

'The County Arcade', stated the Leeds Estates Company brochure of 1903, 'is 375ft long by 18ft wide. It is of magnificent and ornamental design, and undeniably the finest in the country. It contains forty-five shops, an extensive and superbly decorated Cafe Restaurant, and large premises suitable for Furniture or Piano Showrooms or Bazaar purposes . . . The frontages have handsome marble pillars and granite bases. The floor is covered with fine mosaics and the domes are richly decorated with frescos. 'The prettiest Shopping Avenue in the City (*Yorkshire Post*)'. Few who see the Edwardian splendours of the County Arcade today would disagree with its builders' original claims.

By the 1870s the old medieval pattern of streets in central Leeds was totally unable to provide sufficient space for all the shopkeepers who wanted to take advantage of the town's expanding retail trade. One solution was to buy up the old property in one of the yards off Briggate, demolish it, and replace it with a covered street of shops — an arcade. The first Leeds arcade was built on the site of the Talbot Yard by Charles Thornton of the White Swan Varieties in 1877-8. George Smith's Gothic design is reminiscent of a high-naved church, with shop fronts instead of the columns which should support the arches, clerestory windows and vaulted roof.

The famous clock in Thornton's Arcade features Robin Hood, Friar Tuck, Richard Couer de Lion and Gurth the Swineherd from a scene in Walter Scott's 'Ivanhoe'. Every quarter of an hour throughout the day they chime the bells with their fists, a feature which was so popular when they were installed in 1878 that they had to be stopped for a couple of weeks to deter the crowds who came specially to see them in action. A small iron plaque on the back of Gurth is inscribed 'Appleyard, Leeds', indicating that they were carved by John W. Appleyard, sculptor, of 18 Cookridge Street.

In 1899 the Queen's Arcade was built on the site of the Rose and Crown yard, where it provided direct access from Briggate up to the new theatres in King Charles' Croft. Among the plainest of the Leeds arcades, its only decorative feature is the cast-iron railing which surrounds the first-floor gallery.

Named in commemoration of Her Majesty's Diamond Jubilee, the Victoria Arcade was opened in 1898. Designed by Thomas Ambler, it housed twenty-six shops along a glass-roofed L-shaped arcade extending from the Headrow through to Lands Lane, its main entrance having this impressive terracotta façade incorporating Queen Victoria's portrait on a relief roundel above the arch. The arcade was demolished in 1959 for redevelopment as part of Schofield's department store.

By the 1900s, the Queen's Hotel had become recognised as Leeds' premier hotel, a fact confirmed by the quality of its furnishings and decor. The dining-room seen here was refurbished in beautiful white and gold Burmantofts tiling to the designs of C. Trubshaw, the advantages of this material being that it would not absorb the odours of food or stale tobacco smoke, was easily cleaned and hard-wearing, and was extremely pleasing to the eye. What better place to spend an evening, excellent food, a well-stocked bar in the corner, with a balcony above where the musicians could play something light and interesting, perhaps from the latest London shows.

Taking its name from the theatre next door along New Briggate, the Grand Arcade was planned as an 'H' with two parallel arcades of shops and a cross-passage. Smith & Tweedale's design of 1896-97 is quite simple, but a mechanical clock over the Vicar Lane entrance features bell-striking clock-jacks wearing full armour, representatives of the dominions, and a crowing cockerel, all in a Gothic setting which looks more like stage scenery than any real building. Outside, the arcade's street frontages are of Burmantofts Faience, the archways being enriched with polychrome glazes.

The Old Bank Restaurant at 28 Commercial Street was operated by McCaughey's Restaurants and Hotels in the Edwardian period. It was elegantly decorated with parquet floors, panelled walls, and artistic brass electric light fittings. Each table, meanwhile, has its beautifully starched tablecloths covered with cruets holding every condiment the diner could require, napkins laboriously folded into the form of shells, mitres, etc. and either a vase of fresh flowers, or a potted aspidistra. Obviously this was just the place to go for a good businessman's lunch, or for a meal to sustain a vigorous shopping expedition.

The pork butchers of Yorkshire have always enjoyed a splendid reputation for their products, the contents of this window displayed for Christmas shoppers in the 1930s clearly demonstrating their range and quality. Here are hams, succulent stand-pies, some cut in two to show their rich filling, black puddings, polonies, sausages, brawns and decorated 'boars heads'. Inside, the glazed cabinet of table delicacies holds all the mustards, sauces and other relishes which made such excellent accompaniments to the meat.

Situated at No.2 Boar Lane, this branch of Walter Bramham's obviously served a high class of customer, his other shop in the market area offering a rather plainer selection of products.

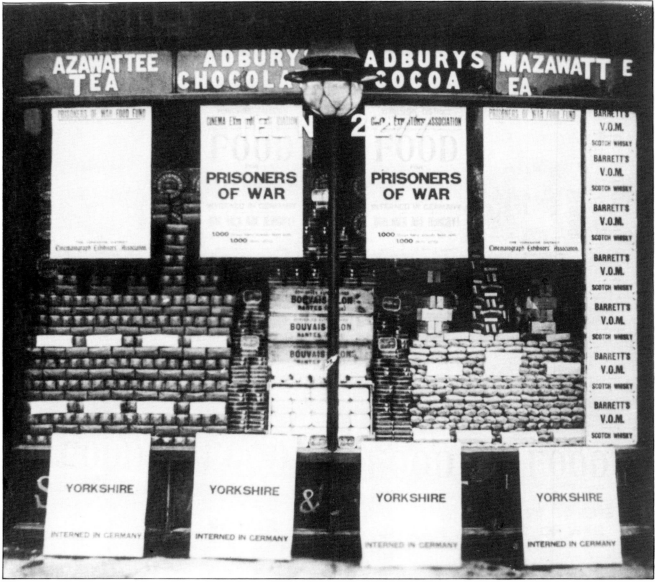

In the early 1940s, this city centre grocer's shop was used by the Yorkshire District Cinematograph Exhibitors' Association to publicise their scheme for sending supplies to Yorkshire soldiers in prisoner-of-war camps in Germany. As the posters stated, 'Our Men are Hungry — 1,000 things have already been sent, 1,000 now going'. The window displays some of them — crates of sardines, boxes of Huntley & Palmer's fruit biscuits, packets of tea, and other basic but essential items.

Opposite page: When the old infirmary buildings on Infirmary Street were demolished, the site was purchased by the Yorkshire Penny Bank for the erection of their new head office and central bank. Perkin & Bulmer of Victoria Square produced this magnificent Gothic design, complete with beautifully detailed gargoyles, and corbels in the form of mythical beasts, angels, etc. The new building was opened with great ceremony by the Duke of Devonshire on 17 August 1894 using a golden key ornamented in appropriate Gothic style. All the local newspapers praised the high quality of its workmanship and design, all of which can still be enjoyed today.

Up to the 1960s, a visit to any of the major Leeds banks was an impressive experience, for their banking halls still retained a wealth of fine architectural detail executed in the highest qualities of material and craftsmanship. Becketts' Bank was superbly Gothic, with a timber roof which would have been a credit to any cathedral, while Alfred Waterhouse's interior of Lloyd's Bank, seen here, used mahogany, mosaic and Burmantofts faience tiling to achieve particularly rich and colourful effects. Regrettably almost all has been destroyed over the past thirty years, only this clock being rescued by the City Museums.

The Leeds and Yorkshire Assurance Company's Office is one of the noblest commercial buildings in the city centre, W.B.Gingell providing admirable façades for the junction of Albion Street and Commercial Street. Built between 1852 and 1855, it admirably demonstrates the quality of the local stone, the plinth being of Bramley Fall, Pool Bank for the rusticated ground floor and Venetian windows, and Rawdon Hill for the upper storeys.

Newly-built in full late Victorian and Edwardian splendour, Park Row boasted a wealth of high-quality commercial architecture. This is the doorway of No.14 — the Hand-in-Hand Fire and Life Assurance Society's Leeds office — which opened here around 1902 on the site of J.Reid & Co's cabinet maker's shop. Regrettably this building was demolished for redevelopment in 1958.

The Old George Hotel stood just to the south of the railway bridge over Briggate. In the thirteenth century it was owned by the Knights Templar, the Templar Crosses beneath the large iron bracket on the inn, and between the top right-hand windows, showing that these properties still enjoyed some of the benefits originally granted to the Knights. In 1847, Charlotte Brontë described its interior, with its figured wallpaper hung with portraits of George II, the Prince of Wales and General Wolfe, its hanging oil lamp, its furniture, mantlepiece ornaments and excellent fire, in *Jane Eyre*.

Here we see it in the tenancy of Mrs Simpson, the last licencee. After her death, the trustee of the owner, a strict Quaker, allowed the licence to lapse and it finally closed its doors on 30 April 1919, being demolished shortly afterwards.

The White Horse, 14 Boar Lane, was one of Leeds' major coaching inns, and from here, every day, the *Royal Union* departed for London, the *True Briton* for Manchester, the *Royal Union* to Harrogate, and the *Hope* to Selby, to meet the steam packet boat which then sailed down the Ouse to Hull. This photograph was taken by E. and J. Wormald around 1869, shortly before all the south side of Boar Lane was demolished for a major road-widening scheme, which converted the narrow medieval street-line into the present broad boulevard, which included a new White Horse.

This photograph shows a block of buildings in Wheatsheaf Yard, which led from Briggate to Lands Lane. They were swept away shortly after 1900 for the construction of Albion Place. In the 1890s, the property on the left belonged to G.Needham of the Leopard Hotel, while the steps on the right led up to the Wheatsheaf's billiard room, where Tom Baker acted as marker. Note the cross just to the left of the Leopard signboard, which could indicate that this was once Templar land.

From the eighteenth century the Cock and Bottle stood on the south side of the Headrow, just opposite its junction with Woodhouse Lane. It was never one of Leeds' major coaching inns, but during the nineteenth century carriers set off from here to make deliveries to Rawdon and Yeadon, and it also provided refreshment for numerous performers at the nearby Hippodrome. In 1938 the inn was purchased by Schofield's, then being demolished, and the site incorporated in their department store.

Today many people are confused by the fact that the Infirmary lies almost a quarter of a mile from Infirmary Street. The street actually received its name from the first Leeds Infirmary, which was built here in 1771 on the site now occupied by the Yorkshire Bank. It was originally designed as a two-storey block by John Carr, the great York architect, but a large wing was added in 1782, and a further wing and a complete additional storey built on in 1786. With 143 beds, it was soon providing services to over 2,000 in-patients and 3,000 out-patients every year. The quality of the care they received from brilliant surgeons such as William Hey made it one of the finest institutions of its kind in Georgian Britain. It was demolished in 1893 to make way for new buildings serving Leeds' growing financial sector.

As Leeds expanded in the nineteenth century, the old Infirmary on Infirmary Street could no longer meet the demands placed upon it, and so a new site was purchased on Great George Street to the north of the Town Hall. Between 1863 and 1867, G.G.Scott produced a splendid Gothic building similar in style to the St Pancras Hotel, on which he was working at the time. Behind the rich façade of brick, stone and polished granite lay a very efficiently planned modern hospital, each ward having lighting and ventilation from both sides, with lavatories, etc. in the corner turrets, as advised by Florence Nightingale. This photograph, taken from the tower of the Town Hall, shows Scott's original three large wings to the left, the matching right-hand wing being added by George Corson in 1891-92.

The wards of the Infirmary were designed in consultation with Florence Nightingale. She recommended that they should have a north-south alignment, with windows facing east and west, and be 16ft to 18ft high, allowing some 2,000 cubic feet of air to each patient. As a result, all the wards were very light and airy, as may be seen from this photograph of the Children's Ward in 1901. It is good to see that the children were encouraged to play by providing such toys as rocking horses, trains, drums and soft toys.

The Exhibition Committee erected this ornate glass and iron roof over the General Infirmary's Central Hall to enable it to be used as a venue for concerts, Sir Charles Hallé conducting here on a number of occasions. This photograph shows it as a combined tennis court and sculpture gallery in 1901, ten years before the roof was finally demolished.

This delightfully informal double portrait shows Sister Porter and Sister Halbert in a brief moment of relaxation at the General Infirmary. Sister Charlotte Porter retired in 1925 after forty-nine years service, while Sister Halbert retired in June 1933 after fifty years. For much of this time she was in charge of Ward Two, where she was held in great awe by medical students!

In the 1880s the Hospital Board decided that it would extend its convalescent facilities by erecting a new hospital for this purpose at Cookridge. Mr and Mrs John North then agreed to donate the necessary cost of the building, £6,000, in memory of their daughter, Ida. The architects Chorley and Connor then proceeded to design the attractive stone, rendered and half-timbered Ida Hospital. It was opened with forty-two beds on 10 May 1888.

The Leeds Public Dispensary was established in 1824 for the purpose of using public subscriptions to provide medical assistance to those unable to afford it from their own resources. From 1865 the dispensary stood at the corner of New Briggate and Vicar Lane, but these fine new premises at Hartley Hill, North Street, were opened by Sir Clifford Allbutt on 12 May 1904. Messrs Bedford and Kitson were the architects, some £33,000 being spent on the erection of the building.

In 1883, the Leeds Fire Brigade moved into these splendid premises in Park Street. Purpose-built at a cost of some £5,000, it included a fire-engine house, guard-room, stable, superintendent's house and office, a joiners shop, a blacksmith's shop, and a tank holding 6,000 gallons of water, which would be extremely useful if the nearby Town Hall or Municipal Buildings ever caught fire. This whole block was swept away for redevelopment in the 1960s, along with the firemen's flats opposite.

This photograph shows the interior of the fire-engine house about 1887, when the third steam-powered Shand, Mason engine had been acquired at the cost of £495. These machines, which were drawn by a pair of horses, used their engines solely to operate powerful pumps which could deliver 900 gallons per minute, and throw to a height of 200ft through a 1⅝-inch jet.

This chemical fire-engine worked on the soda-acid principle used in today's extinguishers. Lightly constructed, it could be rushed to the fire for 'first-aid' treatment, being very successful where a blaze had not already got a good hold. Note the telescopic ladder mounted overhead, the superb quality of the decorative paintwork and the harness suspended from the roof so that it only needed the horses to be placed in position and the hinged collars snapped around their necks to be ready for a swift getaway.

In the 1880s, the City of Leeds Fire Brigade consisted of thirty men: a superintendent, three sergeants and twenty-six constables, all these being members of the police force, in addition to which twelve policemen were held in reserve for fire-fighting duties, who could be called out in an emergency. Here they pose in their new Park Street headquarters, almost everyone sporting a fashionable moustache. The bearded gentleman in the centre of the group is presumably Henry Richard Baker, superintendent of the brigade from 1875 to 1899. Reputed to be a daring driver, he invariably drove the first engine to arrive at a fire and was believed to have attended some 7,000 fires by the time he retired.

On 16 December 1881, approximately one-third of John Fowler's works were destroyed by a fire which started in the middle of the night. It spread with great rapidity, particularly since the company's hoses would not fit on to the town's hydrants. Once the municipal fire brigade arrived, however, it was soon brought under control. Even before the brigade had left, contracts for the rebuilding were signed, and twenty-four hours later an agreement had been reached with the insurance companies. As a result, all the most important parts of the works, including this machine shop, were back in operation within only four weeks.

The Leeds Police were first established in 1815, but it was not until around 1860 that the first purpose-built police stations began to appear around the town, this example being erected at 111 Marsh Lane in 1871. Here we see it just before it was demolished in 1907, with the inspector-in-charge and his staff posing before the door.

Since the Leeds fire brigade and the police were virtually a single body, the mounted police duties in Edwardian Leeds were actually performed by members of the fire brigade, supplemented from time to time by the police. Their main tasks were to control both traffic and large crowds, especially around the city centre. This arrangement was far from satisfactory, however, since the fire brigade could not turn out its engines efficiently if its men and horses were acting as police. The officer seen here was photographed by the City Engineer's Department in 1909.

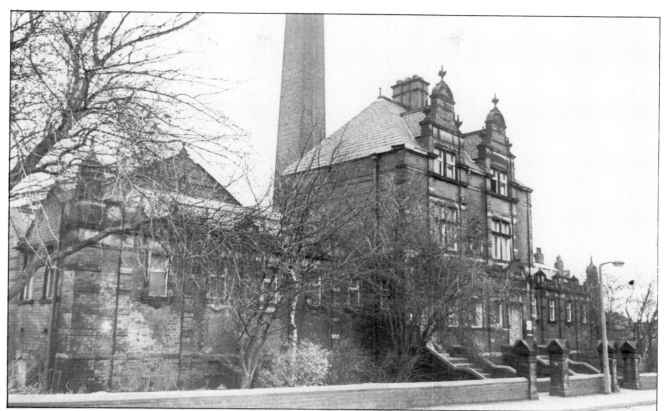

Towards the end of the nineteenth century, the City Council began to build a series of public baths to serve the needs of its populous suburbs. Their standard of construction and design was extremely high, the buildings themselves being of red brick decorated with ornamental carved stonework frequently incorporating the City coat-of-arms. On entering, the vestibules usually had fine mosaic floors and a high screen with double swing doors featuring magnificent stained glass in Rennaisance designs. Then, at the turnstile, the public could pay for the service they required, either a swim in the pool, or a hot bath in one of the cubicles arranged along the front of the building, together with the use of a towel, the fittings of these bathrooms varying according to their class status. Holbeck Baths, opened to the public in 1898, continued in active use up to their closure in 1979.

As part of its social policies of the inter-war years, the City Council built a number of public wash-houses where housewives could have the use of modern machines, dryers etc, thus saving both hard work and damp washing in their own houses. The first wash-house opened in Holbeck in 1928, the Armley wash-house seen here being opened on 27 September 1932, by Prince George. Notice of their closure was issued in 1976, but this had to be deferred following a mass of public protests and a deputation to the City Council. However, the Armley wash-house finally closed on 30 July 1977, when an example of a washing-machine and of a drying cabinet was preserved in the collections of the City Museum.

Up to the 1940s the Aire Valley to the east of Leeds was still a quiet stretch of rural countryside, with hardly a building between Temple Newsam and John O'Gaunt's. Then, in 1947, construction started on the 360-megawatt Skelton Grange Power Station. Over the succeeding years it developed into the massive structure seen here towering over Thwaite Mills, but recently

it has started to reduce in size, one chimney going in 1988 and
the other, accompanied by some of the cooling towers, going
the following year.

In 1893 the Yorkshire House-to-House Electricity Company began the first public electricity supply in Leeds, this undertaking being transferred to the Leeds Corporation in December 1898. The City Electric Lighting and Power Station on Whitehall Road were then greatly extended. Conveyors and mechanical stokers fed coal into a series of twenty-four boilers, the steam being used to power a McLaren and a Bellis engine in the engine-house. This huge room, 220ft by 50ft, also housed the generators which produced up to 8,740 kilowatts. This was sufficient, it was stated, to light over a quarter of a million 35-watt lamps at any one time.

It was probably in the early thirteenth century, with the creation of Briggate, that the first river crossing was established here at Leeds Bridge, although remains of an earlier ford have been found a short distance downstream. The medieval stone bridge, only 12ft wide, was used as the town's first cloth market, the pieces being displayed on the parapet on market days up to 1684, when the clothiers moved into Lower Briggate. After being widened in 1730, 1760 and 1796, it was finally demolished and replaced by the present iron bridge in 1871-3. The channel running into the river from the left is the race from the King's Mills, a short distance upstream.

Victoria Bridge now carries the majority of the traffic which comes into the city from the south. Erected to the design of George Leather in 1837-39, its huge blocks of local gritstone form a graceful elliptical arch 80ft wide, the central block of the parapet being carved with a wreath enclosing the word 'Victoria' in bold capitals. At first tolls were charged in order to recover some of the £8,000 building costs, but these were bought out by the Corporation in 1867.

In order to improve communications at the eastern end of the town, Crown Point Bridge was built in 1840-42 at a cost of £36,000. George Leather & Son designed it as a single 120ft arch of cast iron, all its detailing being in the Gothic style. This, too, was a toll-bridge up to 1868, since which time it has been entirely free of charge. This view looks towards the east, showing Nether Mills and Leeds Lock, the entrance to Clarence Docks being just visible on the right.

Started in 1770, the Leeds and Liverpool Canal is the longest in Britain, its 127 miles climbing 487ft as it crosses the Pennines from the Aire to the Mersey. As the *Leeds Intelligencer* reported on the opening of its first stage in Yorkshire: 'This noble and grand undertaking now affords the most safe, easy, cheap and expeditious method of conveying the produce of different counties to and from the populous manufacturing towns (besides) advancing Agriculture and the Arts of the extensive and populous parts through which it passes and which it ornaments and adorns.' This is River Lock, where the canal leaves the Aire, with the great Leeds and Liverpool Canal Company's warehouse of around 1770.

Although this photograph of around 1900 lacks clarity and is badly scratched, it uniquely captures the atmosphere of the busy life of the River Aire as seen from Victoria Bridge. The steam tug on the left was used to pull barges along the river between the Leeds and Liverpool Canal and the Aire and Calder Navigation, since there was no towpath on this stretch. In the centre, the frames of two barges await completion in the boatyard, while to the right the steam cranes of the Co-op Coal Wharfe empty the barges which had carried their heavy loads from various collieries downstream. The railway viaduct in the background still carries all the main lines from the south and the west into City Station.

The Aire and Calder Navigation provided an ideal means of transporting heavy bulk cargoes into Leeds. *Pioneer* was a sea-going steam vessel captained by Tom Eastwood, a tea and provision merchant from Knottingley. She used to bring flint from the South Coast and chalk from Hessle, near Hull, up the navigation to Thwaite Mills, where she is seen being unloaded by steam crane around 1900.

The River Aire provided a natural and obvious means of transport into Leeds from the East Coast, but it was not until 1699 that opposition from York was finally overcome and an Act of Parliament obtained to make the Aire and Calder navigable. By November 1700, vessels were able to sail upriver as far as Leeds Bridge, to the new 'Town's Warehouse' on the north bank. As trade increased, larger warehouses were required, this magnificent seven-storey block being built in 1827-28. Regrettably, they were destroyed by fire in the 1960s, only their ground floor being incorporated in the recent development of the site.

In 1758, by means of the first Act of Parliament to authorise the construction of any waggonway, or railway, a line was built from the Middleton Collieries, on the southern slopes of the Aire Valley, down to Casson Close, near Leeds Bridge. At first the rails were of wood but, in 1812, cast-iron rails incorporating a rack system were laid to enable two steam locomotives built by Matthew Murray to haul the coal trucks. This was the first practical use of steam traction in the world. These are the staithes at the Leeds end of the line, with Christ Church, Meadow Lane, appearing in the background.

The Leeds & Bradford Railway's Wellington Street Station opened in 1846 on a site immediately behind the present Queen's Hotel. Six years later it was taken over by the Midland Railway, becoming that company's main northern centre and Leeds' major rail terminus. This photograph shows Platform Three around 1910, with businessmen in frock coats and highly finished silk top hats waiting for trains to take them on their respective journeys.

For all general deliveries, the horse and flat-topped wagon provided a cheap and efficient service, particularly around the town. The bales on this example presumably contain paper bags ready for delivery to local shops. For longer journeys, the carriers used the covered wagons, as seen here in Black Swan Yard off Vicar Lane in 1899. This was the traditional base for carriers serving Aberford, Bramham and Horsforth.

The trap provided a very convenient method of transporting either a few people or some light luggage around the district. Probably photographed in the Bramley area in the 1890s, this typical example has the side seats overhanging its elliptical springs, everything about it being beautifully clean and highly polished, suggesting that it was one of the family's newest and most highly-prized possessions.

The Hansom Cab was a prominent sight in the streets of late-Victorian Leeds. Here one trots up Infirmary Street by the side of the Post Office in City Square. This photograph, taken in the early 1890s, also features a group of J.Podesta's ice-cream carts and a marvellous advertisement for Jackson's products:

'Ten little pussy cats been out to dine,
Everyone wearing a Jackson's three-and-nine,
They've all got hats and they don't need suits,
But they ought to be wearing Jackson's Boots!'

The first regular suburban public transport services in Leeds were the horse-drawn omnibuses, introduced in the 1830s. Here we see the omnibus for Beeston Hill standing outside the Royal Hotel in Briggate in 1890. Its proprietor, Charles Joseph Coates, was first granted a cab licence on 1 January 1866. After a brief partnership with his brother, he continued to develop the business on his own, eventually becoming known as one of the best bus proprietors in Leeds, treating both his passengers and his horses extremely well.

This photograph, taken at Leeds City Transport's Kirkstall Road Works in June 1911, marks the end of an era. It shows the last of the Corporation's horse buses just completing its last journey, having returned from the Lower Wortley to Old Farnley route which was now to be served by trolley buses.

When Leeds first began to run motor buses from 1905, it chiefly used them to feed passengers on to the tramways in the Headingley area. This vehicle, U-2379, was made by Tillings-Stevens and entered service on the Moortown-Shadwell route in 1913. Later it was fitted with a double-deck body from one of the 1905 buses, continuing in service in this form up to 1926, when the chassis was sold to W.Cowburn of Hunslet Lane.

Following the passing of the Leeds Tramways Act in 1896, the Kirkstall-Roundhay route was relaid, extended and electrified. Greenwood and Batley, one of the great Leeds engineering companies, manufactured the new cars required for this service, which was officially opened on 29 July 1897. This photograph of 1899 shows one of the brand-new cars standing at Roundhay Park, resplendent in its fine paintwork, tied-back curtains etc.

The first tramways in Leeds began to be constructed in 1871, much of the major development being undertaken by the Leeds Tramway Company between 1872 and 1894. The first trams, all horse-drawn, were made by George Starbuck & Co of Birkenhead. No 34 seen here, was supplied at the cost of £167 on 14 November 1874 and was still in service twenty years later when it was transferred into the City Council's ownership and received its new livery. Its terminus, Reginald Terrace, was at the junction of Chapeltown Road and Harehills Avenue.

In an attempt to reduce costs, the Corporation decided in 1910 to try an experimental trolley bus service between City Square and New Farnley. The official opening took place on 21 June 1911, Leeds having the distinction of being the first operator of trolley buses in Great Britain. Here we see one of the buses standing at the New Farnley terminus around 1912, the old stone building in the background being the Woodcock Inn.

Although the complex junction of tram tracks at the crossing of Briggate and Boar Lane had been re-laid in 1892, they were re-laid once more in 1899, using rails manufactured by Walter Scott Ltd of the Hunslet Steel Works. The paving here was of end-grain wood blocks rather than the usual granite setts in order to reduce the level of noise in these busy streets. This photograph was taken on 10 September 1899, when the new lines had just been set in place.

The tramway system was a source of considerable pride for the Corporation, its success and popularity clearly demonstrating the city's progressive attitude to the challenges of the twentieth century. What could be more natural, therefore, but to choose a decorated tramcar to create one of the most spectacular features of Edward VII's royal visit to Leeds on 7 July 1908. In addition to patriotic greetings, Union Jacks, the city's coat-of-arms, flowers, fringes and bunting, it was fully illuminated by a thousand light-bulbs arranged to pick out the various designs.

At the outbreak of World War One, the tramways were used to promote recruitment into the Regular and Territorial forces. Resplendent in its red, white and blue decoration, this 'Leeds Pals' tram toured the streets to encourage the men of Leeds to report to the Swinegate Tramway Depot for enlistment into the Army, or to Carlton or Harewood barracks for the Territorials. One of the panels on the opposite side instructed: 'Nah then, John Willie, ger agate lad, an' join t'army'. Their destination was quite clear, the indicator board showing 'BERLIN'.

Middleton bogie cars were first run in Leeds in 1935, this example, No 265, being manufactured by English Electric. Most of the small rural village of Middleton was purchased by the City Council for a massive housing scheme which began in 1920. In order to bring in construction materials and also provide a passenger route from the new houses to the centre of Leeds, the Corporation then constructed the 3½ mile Middle Light Railway. The regular passenger service commenced in 1925, when travellers were able to enjoy one of Britain's finest routes as they curved upwards for 300ft through the scenic Middleton Woods, where this photograph was taken in 1956.

The Leeds sculptor E.Caldwell Spruce started his professional career as a modeller at the Burmantofts Pottery Company, but in the mid 1890s he departed for Paris to study in 'some of the most famous studios in that home of Bohemianism and art'. Having returned to Leeds, he set up his studio in Cowper Street, where he produced a variety of modelled and sculpted works. The subject seen here is James Kitson, 1st Baron Airedale, (1835-1911) head of the Airedale Foundry and Monkbridge Ironworks, with their workforce of 3,000 men. He was President of the National Liberal Federation, the first Lord Mayor of Leeds, Honorary Colonel of the Leeds Rifles, and one of Victorian Leeds' leading citizens. Spruce completed this posthumous bust purely from photographs in 1911. It now stands in the entrance hall of the Civic Hall.

The traditional stone-flagged floors of the old Leeds cottages were extremely hard-wearing, practical and cold. Every household, therefore, spent part of the dark winter months making a new hearth rug by cutting old woollen clothes into finger-sized 'clippings' which were then pricked through a piece of coarse canvas stretched on a wooden frame. The resulting rug was very thick, soft and heavy, ideal for the kitchen floor. Plants, situated at the end of Market Street Arcade, had manufactured hand-pricked hearthrugs for sale to those who lacked the time or inclination to make their own since 1863. A similar firm was still operating in Mabgate up to around 1970. From the details shown on this photograph, it looks as if Plants' sold the canvas and clippings for home rug-making, as well as the completed rugs which lie on the bench or hang from beneath the overhanging canopy.

Thomas Milnes ran his joinery business from this first-floor workshop in Bolland Court, Woodhouse Street, around the opening of the twentieth century. Virtually all the processes appear to have been carried out by hand, for no machinery is to be seen, and the walls are hung with veneer cramps, hand-saws and other hand tools. As the mortices in the great tie-beam show, this was originally a timber-framed building, probably of late sixteenth or early seventeenth-century date, which had been encased in brick at some later date. According to local tradition, this room was used for early meetings of the Methodists in Leeds.

Barges were built in Leeds from the early nineteenth century, this dock and dry-dock at the Leeds & Liverpool Canal Basin latterly being operated by William Rider from the early 1880s to 1970. Once the frames had been erected to form the skeleton of the barge, the hull was sheathed in planks, the joints traditionally being packed with oakum, or unravelled rope, hammered tightly into place with caulking tools.

The majority of Leeds' great engineering factories were located in Hunslet, but this did not prevent traditional blacksmiths shops, such as this one on Hunslet Road, surviving through into the 1960s. The guillotine, pillar-drill and belt-driven drop-hammer on the left are all useful labour-saving machines, but the forge on the right, with its hearth, quenching-trough and numerous tongs, is similar to those used by blacksmiths ever since the medieval period.

The Balmforths of Leeds were violin makers of excellent pedigree, Mr Leonard Percy Balmforth (1881-1936) being trained in the craft by Paul Bailly, a pupil of the great J.B.Vuillaume of Paris. He started making violins in Leeds in Cookridge Street around 1906, then moving on to Park Lane, and then Merrion Street. His son, Leonard Geoffey Balmforth (1909-1966), also made several violins, and acquired the reputation of being one of the most reliable experts, scrupulous dealers and connoisseurs of violins in Yorkshire. Here he is seen at work on an instrument, probably in the 1940s.

The village of Bramley has a worldwide reputation for building fine organs, J. & J.Binns Bramley Organ Works, founded in 1880, reputedly being the largest in existence. In 1914 two of their workmen, Fitton & Haley, set up a second organ-building firm here, the two companies merging in 1931 as J.J.Binns, Fitton & Haley Ltd. In order to supply this industry, F.J.Rogers and J.Hinchcliffe started manufacturing and voicing organ pipes in Bramley in 1897, a similar firm owned by F.Horne and S.Wilkinson moving their Yorkshire Pipemaking Company here from Huddersfield in 1925. Today there are still six organ-builders operating in Leeds.

In the 1920s and 1930s, Mr Luigi Tomasso made barrel organs in Leeds. Here he is fixing the pins on the barrel so that the completed instrument can play a selection of dance tunes. They could regularly be heard around the city's streets, being hired out at two shillings (10p) a day in the years after World War One.

Windmills may appear to be out of character with the urban conurbation of Leeds, but seven windmills still survive here, at Seacroft, Colton, Lotherton Lane, Bramham Moor, Hicklam and Kippax Mill Farm. This mill, now known as The Round House, stands at the top of Sugarwell Hill overlooking the Meanwood Valley, only a mile and a half from City Square.

It was once the property of Jeremiah Dixon, who advertised this 'well-situated and good-accustomed windmill to let' in 1775. Up to the end of the nineteenth century there were two mills working here, but then this one was converted into a house in the 1880s, while the other was demolished in the 1930s.

From the early medieval period the site of the recently demolished Queen's Hall was occupied by the King's Mill. Here, by manorial custom, every householder in Leeds had to bring his corn to be ground, the only properties exempt from this 'soke' being those formerly owned by the Knights Templar and the Order of St John, these proving their privilege by displaying a Templar Cross on their front walls.

The rights to the King's Mill and its soke were extremely valuable, Edward Hudson of Roundhay buying them in 1815 for £32,000. In 1839, the Corporation bought up the soke rights for £13,000, thus freeing its citizens from this restrictive burden for ever more. This 1890s photograph looks due south from Swinegate and shows the water taken from the dam under City Station flowing out from beneath the waterwheels of the King's Mills on the right, to disappear under Tenter Lane Bridge on the left. The large block in the background is Concordia Mills.

In 1938 the expansion of the Seacroft housing scheme brought about the demolition of an old flour mill on Foundry Lane. Water from Wyke Beck had been brought here via a channel and a short wooden trough in order to power the mill by means of this waterwheel until its closure in 1912. Mounted on a massive oak axle, cast-iron fittings enabled sixteen radiating wooden spokes to support the iron rim, the whole wheel measuring 30ft in diameter by 4ft 6in in width. Following pressure by local industrial archaeologists, the wheel was dismantled by the Corporation Housing Department and stored at Monkbridge until such time as Leeds developed an industrial museum. By the time this happened, however, the wheel had disappeared, the only evidence for its existence being this photograph and a number of drawings taken at the same time.

Nether Mills, as their name suggests, were the furthest downstream of a whole series of water-powered mills which lined the river and its associated watercourses below the King's Mills. From before 1817 up to around 1840, John Lee used the mills to manufacture carpets, Brussels, woollen and cotton coverlets, and to scribble and slub wool ready for spinning. Then, for the last eighty years of its life, it was occupied by James Richardson & Co, manufacturing chemists, up to its demolition in 1957. Although plans were made to preserve the cast-iron waterwheel, it does not appear to have survived.

Before the introduction of modern synthetic dyes, the woollen industry had to rely on natural materials for its dyestuffs. Some of these, such as logwood and Brazil Wood, arrived from South and Central America and the West Indies in the form of balks of timber which had to be rendered down into small chips before they could give up their colour into the dye-vat. This process was carried out at Thwaite Mills and at a number of other Leeds sites, this particular rasping machine being at Nether Mills.

The first Armley Mills were built to full cloth for the local domestic woollen textile industry in the mid-sixteenth century, the river Aire powering waterwheels which raised great wooden hammers to beat the lengths of wet cloth until they became much thicker and more compact. During 1788-89 the site was rebuilt as the largest woollen mill in the world, but much of this was destroyed in a great fire in 1805. In this photograph we can see, from left to right, the houses erected for the Burrows brothers in 1793, a weaving shed of around 1840, the projecting corn-drying kiln building of 1788-89, and lastly the great fulling and scribbling mill built by Benjamin Gott in 1805, the earliest fireproof building of its type surviving today. In 1982, Armley Mills was opened as the Leeds Industrial Museum, this highly important group of industrial structures being its most superb exhibit.

The first Thwaite Mills started in 1641, but all the present structures were built for the Aire & Calder Navigation Company by Thomas Hewes in 1823-25, at the cost of £15,876. The firm of W. & E. Joy then began to crush rape seed here to make lubricants and oil for lighting, Dyewood and corn were also ground here, but all these activities ceased in 1872 when the Horn family moved to Thwaite. From this time the mills ground flint and china stone for the local pottery industry, barytes for paint, and chalk for use in whitewash, putty, polish and pharmaceuticals. The Horns were forced to cease production in 1976 when a flood carried the weir away, but through the efforts of the Thwaite Mills Society, the mills were preserved and the weir rebuilt so that they are now open to the public as a popular working museum.

In 1792, Benjamin Gott, the great Leeds cloth merchant and manufacturer, revolutionised the operation of this country's woollen textile industry by erecting the first-ever woollen factory on Bean Ing, the area of land between Wellington Street and the River Aire now occupied by the Yorkshire Post building. Here every process from wool-sorting to cloth-finishing could be carried out in the same building, in great contrast to the traditional domestic system. The great mills themselves were built over a period of some forty years, this massive façade facing on to Wellington Street being added around 1829. The whole unique complex was demolished in the 1960s, an inestimable loss to the industrial heritage of this country.

This remarkable building was erected in one of the yards of Benjamin Gott's Bean Ing (Park Mills) in the late 1820s. Measuring 40ft in diameter and surmounted by an iron dome and cupola, it was designed as a gas-holder house, where the coal-gas generated in the gas-house to the left was held in a great iron tank about 30ft in diameter by some 25ft in height. In terms of age and character, these buildings could scarcely be matched by any other remains of the early gas industry in Britain. Even so, they were swept away when the whole site was cleared in the 1960s.

The process of manufacturing woollen cloth started by sorting the greasy and sometimes matted fleece into its various qualities. It was then soaked in warm water and scoured or washed so as to emerge as a soft silky mass of pale cream-coloured fibres. In order to prepare it for spinning, the wool was next passed through a 'willey', which separated any remaining locks and blended it as required, after which it was fed into carding engines, such as these at Armely Mills. As it passed between rollers covered with millions of curved wire points, it was reduced to a uniform film of fibres, which were then condensed into delicate 'slubbings' around an eighth of an inch in diameter.

In order to convert the delicate slubbings into useable yarn, they had to be reduced in diameter and greatly increased in strength by spinning. This process was carried out on the mules, machines which transferred the slubbings from the large horizontal bobbins on top, down between rollers, and on to the hundreds of vertical spindles mounted on the carriages in front. As the carriages ran forward, they drew out the slubbings, spun them into yarn and then wound them on to 'pirns' or bobbins on the spindles on their return journey.

The bobbins from the mules were used in two ways. One half were perhaps dressed with size before being 'warped', that is arranged in order and wound on to a large 'beam' or roller to fit on to the loom. The remainder were wound on to small bobbins which fitted inside the shuttles to form the 'weft'. On power looms such as these, photographed at W.Lupton's Whitehall Mills early this century, the shuttle carried the weft between the warp yarn to produce cloth. Variety in design could be created by selecting appropriate combinations of warp and weft to produce twills, and by selecting different colours of yarns, as when manufacturing tartans, etc.

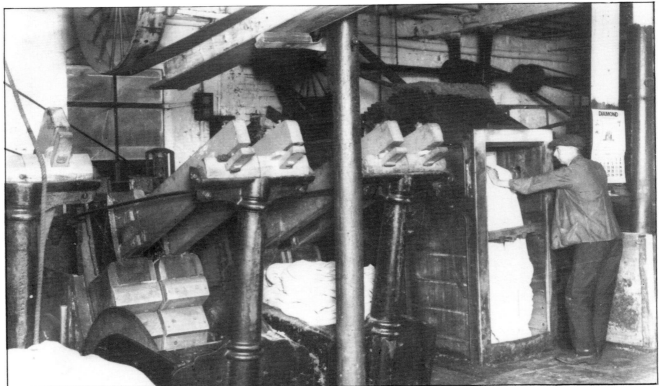

After being woven, the cloth was taken down to the ground floor of the mill to be fulled or milled. These processes caused the fibres of the cloth to become felted together, making it thicker and narrower, and much warmer and weatherproof for the wearer, in addition to enabling it to be cut without fraying. In the fulling stocks, on the left, the wet cloth was processed by being beaten by pairs of enormous wedge-shaped wooden hammers, while in the milling machine on the right pairs of rollers achieved the same effect by squeezing a continuous roll of the wet cloth through a narrow spout. This photograph was taken in Lupton's Mills in 1927.

After fulling or milling, the cloth was fed through the raising gigs, where thousands of French or English teazle-heads mounted in frames on a large cylinder raised a fluffy nap or pile to the surface. As the nap was of uneven length, it then had to be cropped on a machine with spiral rotating blades, the prototype of the lawnmower. Pressing, weighing, measuring and a careful examination of the cloth then followed before the cloth was stored in the warehouse ready for dispatch. Since it was an extremely valuable product, and one which had to withstand prolonged journeys by sea to reach its worldwide customers, packing was extremely important. The bale seen here is being compressed in an hydraulic press and sewn within a protective canvas cover at the Whitehall Mills in the 1920s.

In the early nineteenth century, Leeds became the premier centre of the British flax industry. This was almost entirely due to John Marshall, the son of a Briggate linen draper, who worked with the great innovative engineer Matthew Murray to develop efficient flax-spinning machinery by the 1790s. In 1792, Marshall built his first mill in Holbeck and was already employing over a thousand workers, but as his business expanded, new mill buildings were added in 1794, 1808, 1817, 1826, 1830 and finally in 1838-40, when this vast two-acre mill was built to the designs of David Roberts, as engineer, and Joseph Bonomi as architect. The Egyptian façades, based on the temple of Horus at Edfu, reflect Marshall's interest in Egyptology — he was present at the autopsy of the Leeds Museum's linen-wrapped mummy, for example — but this is only one of this unique building's claims to fame. All the local stories of it being the biggest single room in the world, of it having ducts beneath the floor to provide air conditioning and house the power supply to the machinery, of the chimney being an enormous obelisk, and of sheep grazing the grass-covered roof, are quite true.

Hunslet Mills, Goodman Street, were built in 1838, their entire fireproof construction, with cast-iron columns and inverted T-section beams supporting brick-arched floors, perhaps being the work of William Fairbairn. From 1868 to 1908 they were used by Buckton and May, later Richard Buckton and Sons, for the manufacture of linen bed ticking, towelling, and oil-cloth fabrics, then going into multiple occupancy, housing blanket makers, engineers, leather merchants and manufacturers, and a builder. Although derelict, this fine building still dramatically dominates the Aire & Calder Navigation in Hunslet, but its survival is now dependent on the effectiveness of various preservation organisations.

In the suburbs, where land was much cheaper, the clothing factories built during the twentieth century were usually single-storey. This made the use of lifts unnecessary and enabled the maximum use to be made of natural light. D. Joseph & Sons' factory on Ashton Road, Harehills, was built around 1920 with a typical 'northern-light' roof, the shallow south-facing slope of each parallel gable being covered with slate, while the steeper northern slope was of glass, which thus illuminated the factory floor for the majority of the working hours.

The Leeds wholesale clothing industry, once the largest in the world, was founded in the third quarter of the nineteenth century by the enterprise of two men, John Barran and Herman Friend. The former invented the band-knife and other significant improvements, while the latter devised methods of breaking down the manufacturing process so that it could be efficiently completed by distinct groups of workers, each carrying out a separate operation. Barran's first factory in Alfred Street was succeeded by others in Park Row in 1867, and then by this magnificent Moorish structure, St Paul's House, Park Square, which was designed for him by Thomas Ambler in 1878.

Following the tradition of the local textile mills, the clothing factories erected around the city centre, where land was expensive, continued to be built as tall multi-storey structures. No 91 Great George Street was occupied by J. & N.Campbell, wholesale clothiers, from around 1890; then by Gaunt & Hudson, cap manufacturers and wholesale clothiers, from the early 1900s to the early 1920s; and then by Thomas Marshall & Co, when it became known as Marlbeck House, adopting the name of that company's trademark.

Montague Burton first set up in the retail trade in Sheffield around 1900 but, realising the potential of wholesale bespoke tailoring, he moved to Leeds and set up a small factory at Elmwood Mills. As the business grew, he moved into Concorde Street Mills in 1914, then expanding into four further factories to meet the demand for military uniforms. After World War One there was a renewed boom in the civilian clothing trade and this was accommodated by constructing the Hudson Road Mills in 1920-21. By this time Burton's employed over 16,000 people and were the biggest and most popular clothing firm in the world. This photograph shows the immense Hudson Road workroom.

The Leeds clothing industry consumed vast quantities of cloth manufactured in the West Riding textile towns. Having been transported to the factory, the bales were stored in warehouses such as this one at D.Joseph & Son of Ashton Road. Here they were examined for any faults and measured out on the table in the foreground before being cut to length and sent up to the cutting-rooms.

The cutting-room at C.& M.Sumrie, Ltd, Sumrie House, Leeds 9, in 1943. Having unrolled the cloth, the thin cardboard patterns are being arranged in the most economical manner and chalk lines marked around their edges, so that each piece of the garment can be accurately cut out with the shears.

After seeing a band-saw cutting out multiple layers of wood veneer at an exhibition, John Barran realised that the same process could be adapted for the tailoring industry. The band-knife he introduced in 1858 had a sharp knife-edged blade which could cut up to twenty layers of cloth at once, thus saving an enormous amount of time and energy. Here a band-knife is seen in action at Hepton's in 1947.

By the 1880s the Leeds clothing industry was employing hundreds of workers, many of them Jewish or Irish, in small workshops in the Leylands area around North Street. This Georgian suburb included a number of fine houses, such as the one shown here, which had been split up into a multiple occupancy of living accommodation and workshops. This particular room is being used as a pressing shop for finishing overcoats in the 1940s, before the start of major clearances.

No VIP visit to Leeds was complete without seeing Burton's factory. On their visit on 17 October 1958, the Queen and the Duke of Edinburgh received a tremendous welcome from the workers. Every one of the company's 7,000 employees, 75 per cent of which were women, had a close view of the Royal couple. All the departments were decorated with thousands of yards of red, white and blue trimmings, and most of the women wore colourful favours in their hair. As the Queen and Duke took coffee in the canteen, more than 500 girls entertained them with *Land of Hope and Glory* and *Rule, Britannia*, before Mr Lionel Jacobson accompanied Her Majesty around the factory, as seen here.

Within the Horsforth area a number of quarries provided both crushed grit and building stone for local use from the Rough Rock Series of the Millstone Grit. An added bonus was the utilization of the clays and shales of the overburden to make bricks and pottery. These cranes with their jibs and steam engines pivoting with their vertical shafts are typical of those used in the local quarrying industry around 1900.

The coal seams of the Middleton area of South Leeds were probably worked by means of bell-pits in the late medieval period, then expanding into deeper mines to meet the increasing demands for coal. By the opening of the nineteenth century, Middleton coal was powering numerous factory engines and locomotives, as well as heating thousands of local homes. Here we see the last of the local collieries, Broom Pit, shortly before its closure in 1968. The enormous spoil heaps in the background give some indication of the scale of the underground workings.

Photographs of underground working in the South Leeds collieries are quite rare. This example comes from a lantern slide of 1890 probably taken by Henry Crowther, the Curator of the City Museum, and a specialist in the problems of dust in coal mines. It shows two men drilling a hole into the bottom of the coal face at a Tingley Colliery. When they have finished, the hole will receive an explosive charge packed tightly in place with clay, so that the coal can be blasted free, shovelled into tubs, and pulled along to the shaft. Note their costume: vests, flannel shirts, a double-breasted waistcoat, and woollen or corduroy trousers worn with knee-bands. The safety helmet with its battery-operated cap-lamp was still a thing of the future in mines such as these.

Founded around 1770 by Richard Humble, John and Joshua Green, the Leeds Pottery on Hunslet's Jack Lane produced a wide range of pearl and red earthenwares, and also salt-glazed stonewares. Their most characteristic pottery, the type which most people today think of as 'Leeds-ware', was a very fine cream-coloured earthenware finely cast and thrown into elegant tableware, and covered in a beautiful smooth, glossy glaze. This product sold extremely well throughout both Britain and the Continent, the pattern books having descriptive text in English, German, French and Spanish. During the nineteenth century the pottery changed hands a number of times, eventually closing in 1881. This photograph shows the Time Office at the entrance to the pottery yard, three of the brick-built bottle-kilns being seen in the middle distance. A few years later, a gasworks and other industrial buildings were erected on the site, leaving no trace of Yorkshire's biggest pottery, where some of Britain's finest eighteenth-century wares were produced.

It was in 1842 that the young William Wilcock and John Lassey sank their first mineshaft in the north-east Leeds suburb of Burmantofts, then using the coal and clay they extracted to operate a prosperous brickworks. By the 1870s, four shafts were in production, each with a wooden headstock powered by a steam winding engine. It is recorded that the miners could not be persuaded that the fossils they found were once living plants: 'Tha needn't tell me that tale, for ah'll nivver believe it, them things hev nivver been onnywhear else bud wheear they are now, on' that's wheear God put em!'

Although the Burmantofts works started by making common house-bricks to meet the needs of the growing town, they then began to move upmarket. In the 1870s, salt-glazed bricks began to be manufactured, together with glossy glazed bricks in a variety of colours, of which some 90,000 were made every week. Here we see the glazing room, where the glaze solution was applied to the outer faces of each brick and the surplus brushed off the other faces before they were packed into the kiln for firing.

In 1879 James Holroyd became manager of Wilcock & Co of Burmantofts. A man of considerable energy and vision, he rapidly began to improve both the works and their products. Under his direction a new brickworks was built, and architectural faience, tiles and terracottas developed. This photograph of around 1900 shows one of their chief modellers, E.Caldwell Spruce, at work on a splendid circular cartouche. It was work of this quality that brought Burmantofts its well-deserved national reputation for excellence of design and materials.

The kilns of Burmantofts Pottery in August 1909. Once the wares had been carefully packed inside, the internal loading-doors were bricked up, the coal fires built in the arches stoke-holes, these being carefully tended for a few days until the temperature within rose to around 1,000 degrees Centigrade. The stoke-holes and ash-pits were then blocked, and the whole kiln allowed to cool down slowly for a few days more before its contents could be removed in safety.

William Ingham set up his firebrick works in Upper Wortley in 1825, then trading from 1834 as William Ingham & Sons until amalgamating with the Leeds Fireclay Company in 1886. They made a great variety of architectural ceramics, including bricks, tiles, chimney pots, drain pipes etc, as may be seen in this photograph of their depot at 2 Infirmary Street, in the late 1890s.

The manufacture of clay tobacco pipes began to be practiced in Leeds around 1700, and by the 1850s there were some twenty-three pipe-makers operating here. In 1882, Frederick and Angelina Strong set up their works in Cottage Street off York Road, their son Samson then running it between 1895 and 1950, when he retired. Fortunately, the City Museum was able to rescue much of the Strong family's original equipment, kiln and premises, which were then set up in the Abbey House Museum, where they can be seen today. On the benches in this photograph are the gin-presses used to squeeze the clay into the iron moulds, while on the racks above the pipes dry out, ready for firing in the kiln.

By the late nineteenth century, Leeds had developed into a major centre of the printing industry. The company founded by Alf Cooke (1842-1902) around 1866, occupied first a shop, then a factory, in Hunslet Road. Having built up a substantial trade, disaster struck in 1880 when the works were destroyed by fire. However, a loan of £31,000 from William Beckett enabled him to build a completely new factory nearby and attract sufficient trade to clear all his debts within four years. In 1894 this factory burnt down, too, but in its place rose 'the largest, cleanest, healthiest and most completely fitted Printing Works in the World' all designed by Thomas Ambler. Its clock turret outside is a copy of that on Leeds Town Hall, an appropriate decoration since Alf Cooke was Mayor of Leeds in 1890.

By the 1870s Leeds was the major British centre of the leather trade, the supply of local hides being supplemented by large quantities coming in from France, Germany, Spain, South America and Africa. The largest tannery in Leeds was established on Kirkstall Road in 1828 by Richard Nickols and his partners. Known as the 'Joppa' Tannery, it rapidly expanded to occupy four acres and operate five hundred covered tan-pits, some of which are seen here. Much of the upper leather produced here was supplied to the footwear industry in Northampton, Leicester, the Continent and North America.

The Leeds Steel Works in Hunslet began production in 1889. First the numerous railway trucks in the foreground brought in 9,000 tons of raw materials each week; iron ore from Lincolnshire and Northamptonshire, coke from Durham and Yorkshire, and limestone from Ribblesdale. The blast furnaces processed these into 2,200 tons of iron, most of which was then converted into steel in the Bessemer department, the waste slag being either broken up for road-making, or made into artificial manure. The main products of the works were rolled girders up to 16in x 6in, and tramtracks, of which they were Britain's largest producers. Following their closure in 1934, the works were demolished, so that there is now little evidence of this major South Leeds industry.

By the mid-seventeenth century, water from the thirteenth-century mill-race of Kirkstall Abbey was being used to power an ironworks called Kirkstall Forge, which still flourishes today. Although the forge has expanded massively over the last century, some of the earlier machinery is still preserved *in situ* within its original buildings. When water was fed beneath this waterwheel, it rotated the large cam seen in the right foreground, which in turn raised the massive hammer to the left before releasing it to fall with its full weight on the ironwork placed on the anvil below.

Taken around 1861, this is probably the earliest surviving photograph of John Fowler's single-engine ploughing tackle at work. John Fowler (1826-1864) pioneered the effective use of steam cultivation in the early 1850s, first using a number of manufacturers to build his designs; this engine, for example, being produced by Kitson & Hewitson of Leeds. In 1860 he entered a partnership styled Fowler & Hewitson and set up the Steam Plough Works in Hunslet. From that time, up to the closure of the works in December 1973 'John Fowlers' was one of Britain's greatest agricultural engineering factories, its products bringing into cultivation and increasing the fertility of vast acreages in every continent. Later the company diversified into traction engines, road-rollers, railway locomotive rolling stock, electricity generators, construction machinery, lorries, and a mass of stationary machinery for industrial, mining and plantation use.

The manufacture of electrical generating equipment first started at John Fowler's in 1887, when they commenced experimental work in colaboration with Hanson and Charles of Halifax, and also produced four steam generators for the Royal Silver Jubilee Exhibition at Saltaire. In this photograph female operatives are winding cotton-covered copper cable from the spools at their feet on to formers mounted on the belt-driven lathes. This produces clear evidence of the employment of women in the Leeds engineering industry in the late 1880s.

This enormous engine, the largest colliery winding engine in the world, was supplied by John Fowler's to the Harris Navigation Coal Co Ltd of Treharris, near Pontypridd in South Wales in 1887. Some idea of its scale can be obtained from the great 90-ton steel winding drum, which measured 34ft (10.36m) in diameter. This enabled five and a half tons of coal to be raised from depths of over 2,100ft in under one minute. Heavy engineering of this scale and quality form a great tribute to the achievements of the Leeds engineering industry of last century.

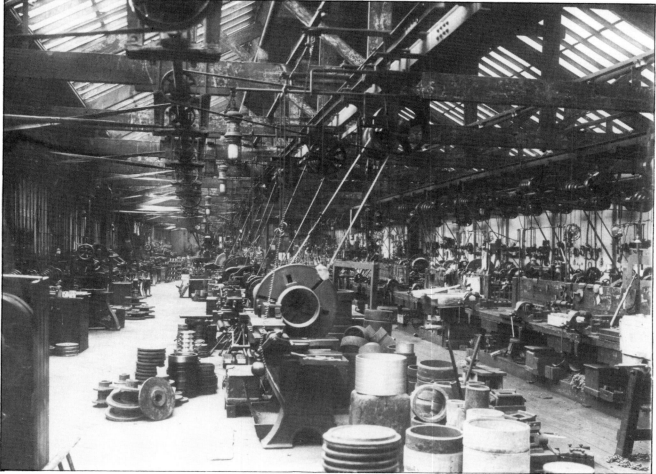

The upper fitting shop at John Fowler's shortly before World War One. Here, as may be seen, pistons and other small components were manufactured using a variety of machine tools belt-driven from the overhead line-shafting. In the early days of the works, a man apparently hanged himself in a small second-floor shop in this department, leading to stories of various supernatural happenings here.

During the Boer War it was discovered that traction engines hauling a number of wagons could move vast quantities of military stores across the Veldt much faster, safer and more efficiently than the traditional ox-carts. In 1900, Lord Roberts, the Commander-in-Chief, ordered four armoured road trains from Fowler's, who were able to design and construct them in only four months. Here the first of these trains is seen undergoing its final test at Methley. As they drove out through Stourton, the driver invited a number of local lads, including my grandfather, to have a ride — so off they went with elder-branch 'rifles' sticking out of the firing loops to shoot imaginary Boers!

The firm of Thomas Green & Son was established in North Street in 1835, where they made everything from pub tables to sausage machines, washing machines, wheelbarrows and even tennis-ball cleaners. One of their major products, however, was the mowing machine. These they sold throughout the world, supplying customers as diverse as the Czar of Russia, the Queen of Norway and the Emperor of Japan, in addition to being given the Royal Warrant as horticultural engineers to Edward VII in 1902. This photograph shows the production line in full flow at the Smithfield Works in the post-war period.

'Tommy Greens' also made locomotives and a range of vehicles for road-making and street-cleaning. This very practical and robust road-sweeper was designed for the company in the opening decades of the present century by W.Porter-Wilkinson. It is seen here in the works yard, freshly painted and ready for delivery. The Smithfield Works closed down shortly after the company was sold to Atkinson's of Clitheroe in 1975. Some of the staff were transferred across to Lancashire, but most remained in Leeds. As one employee commented to the *Evening Post*: 'Many people have given long and faithful service to Green's, but it's been a good company to work for.'

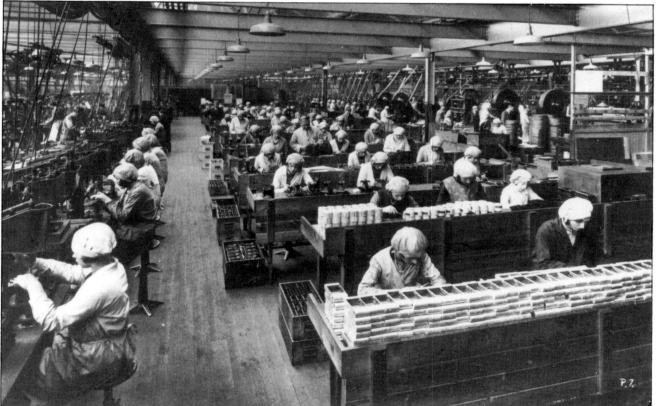

Founded in 1892, the firm of A.Kershaw & Sons established Leeds as a major centre of optical instrument production. In peacetime they concentrated on cameras and 'Kalee' cinema projectors, while in wartime they made gun sights, bomb sights, and binoculars, producing 250,000 of the latter every month in the early 1940s. New factories were opened in Woodhouse Lane in 1910 and in Harehills Lane in 1917, the company continuing to work here from 1948, when it was taken over by the Rank Organisation, through to its closure in 1980. Here the women, who made up to 80 per cent of the workforce, are manufacturing small parts and assembling cameras in one of the large workshops around the 1920s.

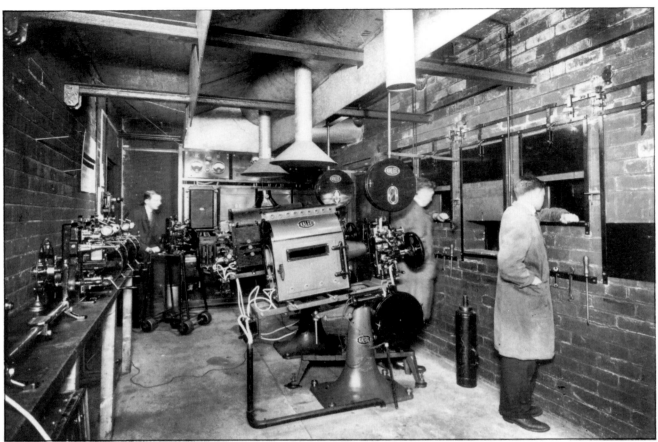

This is the projection room at Kershaws around 1925. In the background a completed projector mechanism is being brought in on a trolley so that it can be fitted on to one of the projectors for testing. Since nitrate film was extremely flamable, all the openings into the room, particularly those down the right-hand wall, were fitted with shutters in order to prevent the spread of any fire which might occur.

Computers, phones, faxes and all the other essentials of office work today are all totally absent from this cost office or general office at Kershaw's. Except for the typewriter, most of the technology of accounting had remained unchanged for a century or more, each clerk working with a steel-nibbed dip-pen, a ruler, and a stand containing red and blue ink to complete the great leather-bound volumes of accounts.

In 1872, Messrs Hathorn Davey & Co purchased the Sun Foundry on Jack Lane and Dewsbury Road, which they re-equipped in order to manufacture pumping engines of the very largest size. One they supplied to the South Staffordshire Mines Drainage was capable of raising 7,500,000 gallons of water from 450ft down every day. In 1936 the company was bought out by the Swiss company Sultzer Brothers and now operates in Manor Mill Lane. Here men are seen working in the foundry in 1899.

The engineering firm of Fairburn Lawson Combe Barbour Ltd could trace its Leeds roots back to Samuel Lawson's Hope Foundry of 1812 and William Fairbairn's Wellington Foundry of 1828. By the opening of the twentieth century it was making high quality textile machinery and machine tools, then, after producing munitions for World War One, it returned to its peacetime work, exporting to America, Persia, China, and the USSR. By 1940 the company was back on munitions, this photograph showing the largely female workforce boring two-pounder gun barrels at their Wellington Street works. Within four weeks of the end of hostilities the bulk of the munitions plant was closed down, and textile machinery began once more to be assembled for export.

Yorkshire ales have had an excellent reputation for centuries, their high quality being highly appreciated both by visitors and by local people, particularly those working in heavy industry in south Leeds. In October 1822, Joshua Tetley (1778-1859) took over William Sykes' brewery in Salem Place, Hunslet. Boosted by the effects of the Beer House Act of 1830, his company prospered and expanded to become the largest brewers in Leeds. By the time Alfred Barnard published his book on *Noted Breweries of Great Britain* in 1889, for which this photograph of the grains courtyard and brewhouse was taken, Tetleys were already the town's major brewer. Barnard was particularly impressed by the 'running ales', 'a good wholesome beverage for the labouring classes; Yorkshire Stingo, very luscious, full of body, and well flavoured without being heady: the light bitter ale, a sparkling tonic and wholesome drink, and finally the East India Pale Ale, for which the firm have such a high reputation in London and elsewhere'. A century later, Tetleys still enjoy the same reputation for the high quality of their products.

It is not surprising that Leeds developed as one of the world's great locomotive-building centres, since it was here that Matthew Murray built the first successful steam locomotive in 1812.

Founded in 1858, Manning, Wardle & Co of the Boyne Engine Works, Jack Lane, Hunslet, were one of Leeds' major locomotive manufacturers, producing engines of various types for use both in this country and overseas. They were awarded the prize medal for locomotives at the International Exhibition of 1862, being praised 'for excellence of workmanship and adaption for the purpose for which it was constructed'.

This is their no.1702, a 0-6-2 side-tank locomotive for the Taff Vale Railway, despatched from the works on 23 July 1906.

Burley Mills were built in 1798-1800 by James Graham, agent to the Earl of Cardigan, for lease to Benjamin Gott, the great Leeds woollen manufacturer of nearby Armley House. The yard was enclosed by this row of eighteen cottages for the workers, each having the stone-mullioned windows typical of weavers' housing in this region. The central gateway and office block, seen on the left, has a clock made by James Prince, its bell being mounted in an octagonal cupola above, which was originally crowned by a weather-vane featuring the figure of a goat. The block in the distance was used as a weaving-shed for the blankets made here, the main building, out of view to the right, being used for the scribbling and spinning processes.

Matthew Murray (1765-1826) was one of the Industrial Revolution's most creative engineers, his developments ranging from the world's first practical steam locomotive, to spinning machinery, machine tools and engines. In 1804 he built this house on the site of the present Holbeck triangle of railway lines just to the west of the City Station. Officially entitled 'Holbeck Lodge', it was more popularly known as 'Steam Hall', since Murray had equipped it with a steam central-heating system, a century and a half ahead of its time.

During the massive expansion of Leeds as a commercial and industrial centre in the nineteenth century, virtually every available building plot within a mile of the town centre became occupied by factories and workers' housing. By 1914, half the houses were over seventy years old, many of them being in an appalling condition due to the piecemeal development, overcrowding and a lack of ventilation, drainage, sanitation and maintenance. From the 1870s the Corporation began a series of compulsory clearances, fortunately recording many of the properties beforehand by means of photographs. This is Atack Place, off Cross Billet Street, in the Quarry Hill area. The dapper gentleman is not a local resident, but one of the surveyors who often appeared in these views.

Copenhagen Street stood where the Inner Ring Road now crosses North Street. Like the adjoining Trafalgar Street and Nile Street, it took its name from one of Nelson's victories, these still being a matter of some celebration when it was laid out by Mr Bischoff in 1809. By the time this Edwardian photograph was taken, every trace of its former rural environs had totally disappeared. Now it was a narrow inner-city street, one side being lined with small cottages, while the other houses the privies, outbuildings and yards of the properties fronting on to Trafalgar Street.

Having purchased McAndrew's Garden in 1787, the Leeds property developer Richard Paley sold it off in plots to sub-developers, such as Mr Riley, who then built this narrow court of fourteen backside cottages. The only entrances to Riley's Court were the tunnels leading from York Street to the north, and Off Street to the south. By 1832 the court was already being described as confined, dirty and overcrowded, with seven of its inhabitants infected with cholera. This situation was certainly not improved by the building of the railway viaduct in 1865-69, but even so, people continued to live here within the present century.

In most large industrial cities, local byelaws of the 1860s had banned the erection of back-to-back houses. In Leeds, however, it was only thought necessary to insist that a privy-and-ashpit yard should be provided between each block of eight. Although an Act of Parliament of 1909 demanded that no more back-to-backs should be built, it still allowed the construction of those which had already been approved, thus allowing Leeds developers to continue building them up to 1937. Whatever the sanitary reformers believed, most local people found their combination of cellars, kitchen/living room and scullery, and a number of bedrooms, to be convenient, warm and comfortable. This is Stanley Terrace, built in Armley in the 1890s.

In 1901 a private developer built one of the first inner-city rehousing schemes on Woolman Street, not far from the Parish Church. Described as 'tennement dwellings', they were three-storey blocks of flats, arranged in groups of twelve and fifteen separated by staircases which access to the open galleries. The architect apparently had an interest in local vernacular styles, for each door and window lintel were carved to resemble those of seventeenth-century Pennine mansions, while all the windows were sideways-sliding Yorkshire sashes.

The congested mass of small brick-built cottages and narrow yards that occupied much of the Quarry Hill area were a matter of serious concern to the city's Unhealthy Areas Committee. In 1906 they obtained the consent of the Local Government Board to allow the removal of 2,000 people from Quarry Hill, the first demolitions including the worst areas of housing, and the lines of two proposed streets, as seen in this photograph. It was not until the 1930s, however, that the whole site was cleared ready for building the Quarry Hill Flats.

While searching for positive solutions to Leeds' housing problems, a group of West Riding architects and housing committee members visited Karl Ehm's *Karl-Marx-Hof* unified development of apartments, shops, launderies and kindergartens in Vienna, where they were greatly impressed by its scale and fine humanised architecture. A further visit to the *Cité de la Muette* at Drancy in France then demonstrated the structural system of precast cladding mounted on a steel frame developed by Eugene Mopin. Using these elements, the Director of Housing, R.A.H.Livett, designed Quarry Hill, the biggest block of flats in Europe. Its vast range of rectangular and curving blocks enclosed a range of communal facilities, all set on a sloping site rising from the astern end of the new Headrow and Eastgate roadway. Built between 1935 and 1941, it provided accommodation for 3,280 people up to its demolition in 1975-78.

The laundry at Quarry Hill was situated over the Garchey waste station, the housewives having to haul their prams, etc. loaded with curtains, bedding and other washing up a series of thirty-eight steps. However, once there they entered the real social centre of the complex, where amid the din of the machinery and the hot, steamy atmosphere, issues such as tenants' rights were discussed in detail. This photograph of around 1940 shows the laundry equipment in the foreground, while against the back wall are banks of sliding racks where the washing was dried by hot air.

The first municipal housing policy in Leeds started in 1919, just after the end of World War One. Concrete houses were first tried at Crossgates and Meanwood, but then the City Council returned to traditional methods of construction. This photograph shows a typical group of Leeds council houses on the Wyther estate in June 1921, shortly after they had been completed. Such features as the arched window heads, the corbelled eaves to the gables, and the circular windows all helped to give them an attractive appearance.

The original kitchens at Temple Newsam were probably in the south-east corner of the house. In her remodelling of 1792-96 the widow of the last Viscount Irwin constructed this impressive new kitchen in the basement of the north wing. It was 240ft from the dining-room, access for the food being along a dark and narrow subterranean passage running beneath the courtyard. In this photograph we see the kitchen as it was displayed to the public in the inter-war years. At this time the estate fire-engine was shown here, a hand-powered model acquired from Hadley & Sons of London in 1822.

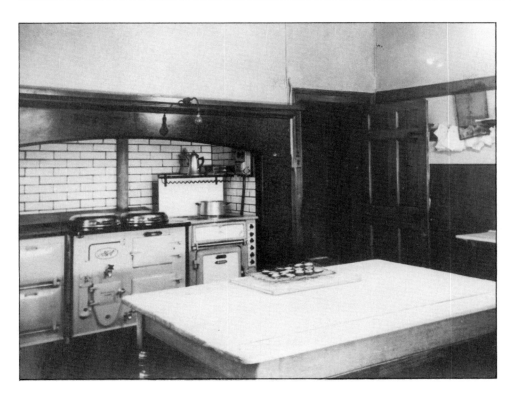

When this kitchen at Farnley Hall was first established in the nineteenth century, its wide stone fireplace would have been filled by an enormous black-leaded iron cooking range, complete with an open fire for roasting and ovens for baking. By the 1930s, when this photograph was taken, it had been refitted with much more convenient solid-fuel Agas which maintained ovens, hobs and hot water for ready use. The electric cooker provided additional hobs, oven and grill which could be brought into use simply by turning a knob, a great improvement on the old coal-fired stoves of earlier years. Apparently baking has just finished, a tray full of small cakes being set on the table to cool.

This wash-kitchen, complete with its stoneware sink, set-pot or copper and fireplace suitable for housing a Yorkshire range, also doubled as the family bathroom. Sat before a glowing fire, with hot water ladled out of the set-pot, warming towels on a clothes-horse providing an efficient draught-screen, the tin bath could be an extremely pleasant and comfortable experience, unless one touched the hot side of the bath nearest to the fire! Afterwards the water might be ladled down the sink, or the whole bath could be tipped out over the flagstones in front of the house, so that they could be scrubbed and swilled to perfect cleanliness.

This scullery in a Victorian back-to-back was typical of thousands of others which survived in Leeds up to recent times. On the left is the set-pot or copper, an iron cauldron set in a masonry hob. Once the fire beneath had been lit with paper and sticks and then stoked with coal, it soon heated the water to boiling point. Note the enamel ladling-can on top, ready to bale the water into a wash tub, or perhaps a tin bath. The stoneware sink on the right provided a large flat area where washing could readily be scrubbed, the vegetables prepared and the washing-up done in enamel bowls, the cupboard beneath being useful for storing bleach, washing soda, and similar necessaries. As seen here, most households managed to arrange a gas-ring or two around the sink. They were much cleaner and more efficient than cooking over the coal fire in the living room, as well as permitting cooking to be carried out without lighting the fire on hot summer days.

This Yorkshire Range is typical of those installed in Leeds terrace houses from the early nineteenth century through to around the 1920s. They were extremely practical and efficient, providing heat for warming the living room, for cooking and baking, for providing hot water and for drying and airing clothes. In addition, the flickering flames and glowing coals of its fire made it the real focus of family life, even though polishing the black-leaded ironwork, emptying the flues, heaving up the buckets of coal and cleaning up all the dust and ashes provided a constant source of work.

The sculleries in the Quarry Hill flats were equipped with the Garchey method of water-borne refuse disposal. Waste materials were placed in the refuse hopper beneath the sink from where, after a plunger had been lifted, as seen here, it was flushed down a waste stack and on to the disposal station, where it was collected, dehydrated, and burned. The remainder of the fittings, including the pot-shelf and cup-hooks, the draining board, the work-tops on which gas-rings could be mounted, and the fitted cupboards beneath, were all good design and materials for this period.

The great hall at Temple Newsam has occupied the southern wing of this great rectangular house ever since it was built, probably between 1500 and 1520. Since that time it has been remodelled on a number of occasions, particularly in the 1790s, and the 1820s. This photograph of around 1910 shows its fabric in its final late Regency form, which is still to be seen today. Note the magnificent billiard table with its appropriate 'Jacobean' legs, and also the brass cannon beneath. These were acquired by the Ingram family around 1700, and still decorate this imposing room.

The Picture Gallery, a magnificent room measuring 108ft by 28ft, is one of the finest interiors in the North. It was remodelled for the seventh Viscount Irwin in 1738-45, the ceiling being decorated by Thomas Perritt and Joseph Rose of York, the doorcases were probably by Richard Fisher, another York craftsman, while the monumental chimney pieces were based on designs by William Kent. This photograph of around 1910 shows the gallery set out in the crowded Edwardian manner. Much of the later soft furnishings have now gone, but visitors can still see the exquisite suite of gilt wood and needlework chairs, settees and day-bed made for this room by James Pascal of London in 1746, and the gilt girandoles of 1750, attributed to Matthias Lock of London, which hang from the left-hand wall.

The so-called Darnley Room at Temple Newsam is shown here after its redecoration for the visit of the Duke and Duchess of York in 1894. The celebrated Stork wallpaper seen in this photograph was covered over only two years later, when the walls were encased in Jacobean Revival panelling and plasterwork. In another room, however, the same design survived through to the 1940s and has recently been reprinted.

In the years after World War One, many of the large houses began to replace their rather heavy over-furnished Victorian interiors with others of a more relaxed and comfortable atmosphere. This is the drawing-room of Farnley Hall, Old Farnley, the home of the Armitage family up to the mid-1940s. With its vase of fresh flowers, chintz-covered easy chairs, convenient tables for drinks, a telephone, and electric lighting, it looks to be an ideal place for the more informal lifestyle of the 1930s.

In the 1830s, Dr Baker discovered people living close to the Parish Church 'in dark and dank cellars, including pigs, with broken panes in every window frame, and filth and vermin in every nook, with the walls unwhitewashed for years, black with the smoke of foul chimneys, without water, with corded bedstocks for beds, and sacking for bedclothing, and with floors unwashed from year to year'. Cellar dwellings were still in use in the 1890s, this extremely rare photograph showing the interior of one in Mushroom Street.

Inside the Quarry Hill Flats, the living rooms were very simply finished with narrow ceiling cornices, lengths of picture-rail on the walls, a metal rod for the window curtains and a very limited number of power-points. The fireplace, meanwhile, was fitted with two swivelling stands, on which kettles or pots could be heated on the fire. Within this basic shell, it was possible to create a very comfortable and fashionable interior, as proved by this photograph. Note the typical three-piece suite with its contrasting silky cushions and antimacassars, the stained oak sideboard, table and chairs, and the opaque glass light fitting.

Not everyone wished, nor could afford, to completely refurnish when they moved into Quarry Hill Flats, and so they brought in the furniture they had used in their old homes. As in many other West Riding households, the sideboard, table, chairs and pictures were good-quality survivors from those more prosperous years before World War One. The bottle of milk with its wide neck sealed by a cardboard disc, the 'Tit-Bits Sauce' and, 'Tizer — The Appetizer' were regular accompaniments to most meals around this time.

Founded in 1819, the City Museum has always played an important part in the life of the city. Situated halfway down Park Row, on the site of the present Midland Bank, it had its original Greek Revival premises greatly enlarged and remodelled in the fashionable Italian style in 1861-62 by the Leeds architects Chorley & Dobson. One of its major features was a fine lecture hall with curved rows of seats rising one above the other in the form of a Greek theatre. Speakers ranged from Flinders Petrie and Mortimer Wheeler to Anthony Trollope, Matthew Arnold, and William Morris, while the performances given by Frantz Reizenstein, Isobel Baillie, Myra Hess and Owen Brannigan thrilled the audiences here, particularly during the wartime concert seasons.

Around 1825, John Calvert, a Leeds gunsmith, bird and animal preserver and dealer in foreign and fancy birds, moved into this property on the junction of Lands Lane and Commercial Street. He then proceeded to brick-up the windows of the upper storeys to create a 54ft by 36ft top-lit museum gallery to house his 15,000 natural history specimens. Part of the display featured 'a large and interesting cavern or grotto, composed of about three tons of Virgin Cork Bark, with lamps and appliances for fountains and waterfall designed by Mr Taylor of Leeds and London'. Regrettably this great collection was sold off in 1874, this photograph showing the building just before its demolition around 1900.

This gallery in the City Museum was built in 1820-21 and then remodelled with the mezzanine walk-way and roof-lights in 1826. At the opening of the twentieth century it was used to display the museum's magnificent collection of birds which had been gathered from virtually every part of the world. It was an extremely popular venue for both local people and for visitors from elsewhere, no trip to Leeds being complete without a visit to the museum to see the great Bengal tiger, the Egyptian mummies, the massive wild yak, and numerous other spectacular specimens.

The museum's zoology gallery was a classic of its period, a vast room filled with magnificent specimens from the animal world. In the foreground are the legs of the mighty Irish elk with antlers over 13ft across, collected from Lough Gur in 1847, then a walrus skeleton of 1868, and the skeleton of an elephant which had formed part of Wombwell's Menagerie until the animal's death in 1841. Many Leeds people today can remember walking round the raised gallery, marvelling at the thousands of exotic butterflies, the intriguing specimens preserved in jars of spirit, and many other delights. Regrettably, all these were put in store when the site was sold for redevelopment in 1966, and the museum moved into its present temporary accommodation.

Leeds was a great pioneer in the field of museum education, especially during the curatorship of Henry Crowther from 1893 to 1928. From the 1890s, parties of children from the local board schools were received in two weekly batches of around 350 delivered by the Leeds Tramways. A lantern-slide lecture was then given by the curator, each child being given a printed syllabus outlining the content of the lecture, and those specimens which should be studied in the museum. They then split up into groups to see the actual exhibits, before returning by tram to their schools for further study and essays describing what they had seen and learned. By the time of his retirement, Henry Crowther had taught an estimated 500,000 children and 12,000 teachers, a record which probably remains unbroken today.

As the post-war clearances of the narrow yards of old workshops and cottages progressed, the City Museum began to collect examples for preservation at the Abbey House Museum. They were re-erected in a new extension called 'Abbey Fold', which was opened in July, 1954, by Dr Sherwood Taylor, Director of the Science Museum. Visitors were now able to 'step back in time' to see a blacksmith's shop from Horsforth, a saddler's shop, a handloom weaver's, a worker's cottage, etc. all constructed and furnished with locally collected material. To mark the opening, this group of students from Leeds Univeristy came down to pose in costume for the benefit of the local Press.

In the 1890s, the City Art Gallery built up an extensive collection of casts taken from some of the finest examples of sculpture to be found anywhere in the world. Many were copied from originals in the British Museum, the Louvre, the Vatican, from Florence, Berlin, etc. Their purpose was to promote popular interest and knowledge of sculpture, George Birkett, the curator, preparing a 46-page guide which enabled the visitor to follow the history of this subject from Ancient Egypt through to the present day. Here the casts are seen on display in 1911 in the magnificent Sculpture Gallery on the ground floor of the Municipal Buildings, a room now changed beyond all recognition in order to house the Commerical and Technical Library.

On 8 July 1840, a company of shareholders opened the Leeds Botanical and Zoological Gardens on land on both sides of the present Cardigan Road between Burley and Headingley. There were to be all kinds of plants, wild birds and animals, the bears being kept in this castelated bear-pit, which still stands at the side of the road. The project was not a success, however, and in 1848 the gardens were taken over by 'Tommy' Clapham, who continued them as pleasure grounds for a further ten years, before moving on to establish his 'Royal Park' nearby. Cardigan Road was then created and the gardens split up into individual building plots.

The Leeds Library, the oldest proprietory library in Britain, first opened its doors to members on 1 November 1768, in order to satisfy the Leeds gentry's growing interest in the fields of science, technology, travel, history, theology and literature. On payment of a subscription of one guinea (£1.05) plus five shillings (25p) each year, members could borrow books from the stock selected by a committee. In 1808 the library moved into these purpose-built premises on Commercial Street. Designed by Thomas Johnson, they incorporate four shops at street level, their rental helping to finance the operation of the library above.

Inside the Leeds Library, the gallery, staircase and bookcases still retain their original appearance. Here, in March 1884, just as the librarian, A.J.Edmunds, was about to leave at the end of the day, he saw an old man with a pallid face and deep-sunk eyes amid the bookcases. Thinking him to be a burglar, Mr Edmunds took his revolver from the safe and pursued the intruder, only to find that the figure simply disappeared before him. On describing this incident to the Revd Hargrove next day, he was told, 'Why, that's old Sternberg!', the librarian from 1867 to 1880. Further supernatural events continued until the following April, but since that date he appears to have remained at rest.

In 1871, the Corporation had adopted the Public Libraries Acts, it set up its first premises above a block of shops in Infirmary Street, the reference section being at the front, with the lending library to the rear. When the new Municipal Buildings were erected in 1884, they incorporated this magnificent reference library on the upper floors. Its design is loosely based on a medieval great hall, completed with a gallery and a dais canopy over the bookcases, while to create an even greater impression of space, the end gables are clad in mirrors to reflect the lines of the deeply-coffered timber roof.

The borough of Leeds opened its first lending library in October 1870, and within a few years a number of active branches were in operation, one being in the Providence Sunday School in Armley. In 1898 the Library Committee decided to erect a new library in Armley, choosing a design prepared by Deny Robinson. The same architect was responsible for all the interior decoration, a the furniture, the leaded lights, and the air-conditioning provided by a water-fan in the clock-tower. When Cllr John Bowling opened the library on 17 April 1902, he was able to claim it as the first building erected by the city purely for library purposes, and the first of an extensive series which still serve the people of Leeds today.

Hunslet Moor, a straggling common of 68 acres, was formerly used for knurr and spell, cricket matches and similar local sports. In 1879 the Corporation purchased the rights to the Moor, and proceeded to make it into a public park, complete with ornamental flower-beds, a bandstand, shelters, a circular pond called 'The Lake', and walks illuminated by lamps hung from archways. To commemorate these works, William Emsley presented this magnificent drinking fountain, turret clock, weathervane and lamp in 1880. Note the Leeds coat of arms proudly displayed on each side.

Elephants, howdahs, elaborate processional carts, magnificently costumed performances and a group of villagers of all ages — in fact, a complete Ceylonese community. They appear to be quite out of place in a book about Leeds, but clues are provided by the buildings which appear hazily in the background. Behind the elephants, for example, rises the spire of St Augustine's, Wrangthorne, for this is Woodhouse Moor. In the 1880s a promoter brought this group here, complete with all its wooden houses and domestic equipment, as part of a nationwide tour. The people of Leeds were enthralled by the colour and spectacle of the dancers, but thought very little of the accompanying music, since it was quite beyond their own range of experience.

When first built to the designs of Cuthbert Brodrick in 1866-67, the Oriental baths really were oriental, with coloured bands of brickwork, doors, windows and parapets in an elaborate Indian style, all beneath a cluster of bold domes and a soaring minaret. In 1882, all this delightful frivolity was swept away when the baths were enlarged and remodelled in this stern Gothic manner by William Bakewell. The City Council operated the baths here between 1898 and 1967, when they were closed for demolition. Fortunately the Museum was able to rescue the statue of a lady in her Victorian bathing dress who used to appear as if diving into the middle of Cookridge Street from her Gothic niche!

The Canal Gardens at Roundhay were constructed when the park was still in the private ownership of the Nicholson family. The 'canal' itself is a purely ornamental sheet of water measuring 350ft by 45ft, the rustic stone bridge seen in the distance carrying a broad walk which proceeds around the whole garden. This photograph, by Wormald of Leeds, shows the appearance of this popular area of the park some time in the third quarter of the nineteenth century, when it had just been newly planted.

No early nineteenth century landscape was complete without a suitable temple or Gothick ruin. In 1821, Thomas Nicholson of Roundhay employed George Nettleton to construct this romantic castle overlooking his extensive woods and lakes. In the room over the gateway, lunches were served to pheasant-shooting parties, while at other, quieter times, it made an idyllic sewing room for Mr Nicholson's daughters. It must have provided the ideal atmosphere for reading Sir Walter Scott's latest works. Here it is seen in the 1860s, before the Corporation stripped the ivy, inserted new windows, etc.

The waterfall at Roundhay Park, photographed in the 1890s. This romantic feature, constructed from huge blocks of gritstone, measures over 60ft in height. The rock in the centre of the two rustic bridges across the top was locally known as the Lover's Leap. It had to be removed after a number of people attempted to commit suicide by jumping from its flat top.

The Waterloo Lake at Roundhay Park provided the residents of late Victorian Leeds with the opportunity to enjoy either rowing in small boats, or sailing in yachts, just as if they were on the fashionable waters of Windermere. The steam yacht *Maid of Athens* was replaced in 1899 by the electric launch *Mary* *Gordon* named after Mrs Gordon, Lady Mayoress in that year. Here the vessel is seen carrying passengers who had paid tuppence each, a penny if aged or under twelve, on a summertime cruise, one of the many she completed before being sold in the early 1920s.

To mark the opening of the new General Infirmary at Leeds, it was decided that the whole building should be used to house a National Exhibition of Works of Art. It was an extremely ambitious project, involving the borrowing of vast numbers of specimens from the Royal Family, from private owners and from the South Kensington Museum. The exhibits included 3,587 fine paintings and engravings, 3,208 specimens of decorative art, and 393 examples of Indian art, all these being listed in a 344-page guidebook.

This commemorative photograph of the directors and officials was probably taken around the time of the opening on the 19 May 1868, by the Prince of Wales. By the time it had closed at the end of October, the exhibition had proved itself to be a great success, having attracted 568,780 visitors.

Having been fully restored by the City Council in 1890-95, Kirkstall Abbey and its grounds were laid out as a public park, complete with gravelled paths, park benches, a bandstand, a row of slot machines, a large area which could be flooded for skating in the cold winter weather, and, just as important, a series of large notice boards listing all the appropriate City

Council Byelaws. This photograph records a religious festival in the Abbey grounds around 1900, when the newly-planted trees still retained their original modest proportions, and the Abbey itself still dominated the site.

The general public have always been given access to Kirkstall Abbey, its private owners allowing anyone to study the ruins, or enjoy the grounds for picnics and quiet recreation. This group of children may have come here with their Sunday School, for they are too few in number, and probably too well-dressed, to have come from one of the larger Leeds Schools. At this time, in the 1880s, John Octavius Butler had the lease of the site and was carrying out important structural repairs. For this reason James Wardell dedicated his excellent guidebook to him. Its 92 pages contain a wealth of observation and historical detail of the Abbey, as well as a poem extolling its beauty:

'Where holy monks devoutly prayed
And told their beads the while,
The wintry wind with ruthless blast
Sweeps down each lonely isle . . .

Though each attractive scene is gone,
Which graced its former day —
Yet still the venerable pile
Is lovely in decay.'

Gardening, both for vegetables and for flowers, was a very popular recreation in Victorian and Edwardian Leeds, numerous amateurs producing impressive results from their gardens or allotments. Great efforts were made to achieve success in the local flower shows, such as this one held at Crossgates in 1905. Note the impressive display of dahlias on the table.

The gardens and parkland around Temple Newsam have always been one of its chief glories. In the seventeenth century the areas around the house were set out in the formal patterns fashionable at that time, but these were largely swept away when the whole park was landscaped by Lancelot 'Capability' Brown in the 1760s and 1770s. Further formal gardens, including this beautifully manicured example, were created around 1875, their symmetrical arrangement of large urns and beds of colourful plants all being arranged around a central fountain. This view was taken from the south terrace around 1908.

The packed audience is all in Victorian costume, the lights dim and the immaculately dressed Leonard Sachs rises from his chair to call, "Good Evening, Ladies and Gentlemen!" As millions of television viewers will remember, these words introduced the immensely popular *Good Old Days* programmes televised from the stage of the famous Leeds City Varieties. Built in 1865 by Charles Thornton of the White Swan Inn, Swan Street, this intimate theatre still retains its original auditorium, complete with stalls, first-floor boxes, and second-floor gallery. The bar is worth seeing, too, particularly for its fine collection of autographed photographs left by the numerous famous performers who have appeared here over the past century. Probably no other theatre so accurately preserves the atmosphere of the traditional English music-hall.

There are very few visual records of the artistes who entertained the crowded audiences of the Leeds variety theatres and music halls of Victoria days. This remarkable act, seen against the painted background of a photographer's studio, comes from a collection of Leeds lantern slides of around the 1890s. Whatever the quality of the performance, the cut of the suit is certainly a most impressive example of tailoring craftsmanship.

For many Leeds people, the Theatre Royal provided their first ever experience of a theatrical performance, for it was the centre of the city's pantomime tradition. Even in the 1860s the Royal Amphitheatre had boasted the best transformation scenes, but its greatest successes were the pantomime seasons promoted by Francis Laidler between 1909 and 1957. Public support was so great that they frequently ran for up to twenty-two weeks, far beyond the Christmas season. Regrettably, all this ceased in 1957 when Schofield's bought the theatre for demolition in order to enlarge their store.

The Theatre Royal, King Charles Croft, was opened on 2 October 1876, seven months after its predecessor, the Royal Amphitheatre, had been burnt down. Outside, it was decidedly dull and boring, but inside it had a splendid atmosphere, being one of the city's favourite theatres. Thomas Moore & Sons designed it to hold 4,000 people in the stalls and the ascending tiers of galleries. They faced this ornate proscenium decorated with a moulded composition called *carton-pierre*. Note the Leeds coat of arms placed over the centre of the stage.

In order to provide Leeds with a 'magnificent temple of the drama', a limited company commissioned the successful local architect George Corson to design a new theatre for an extensive site on New Briggate. Much of this work was actually carried out by his chief assistant, James R.Watson, who had particular knowledge in this field. Using a blend of brickwork with stone dressings, typical of Leeds buildings of the late nineteenth century, they produced this fine frontage in the Romanesque manner. The audience which entered the theatre on its opening night, 18 November 1878, can have had little idea of the sumptuous facilities inside, these including an assembly-room to seat 1,200 and a large supper-room, in addition to the theatre itself.

In 1878, the auditorium of the Grand Theatre was considered to be one of the finest in Europe or America, good views of the stage being obtained from all the 2,600 seats, and from the 200 additional standing-places. Virtually every surface, the proscenium, the ceiling, and the fronts of the dress, upper, and amphitheatre-circles were richly decorated in moulded *carton-pierre*. Gothic fan-vaults and clustered columns, along with Italionate scrolls, brackets and roundels and rich formalised foliate motifs all combined to create the most impressive atmosphere of opulence and grandeur. Today it remains one of Britain's finest theatres, providing an appropriate home for English National Opera North.

From the early fourteenth century, or even earlier, Leeds Fairs were held twice a year, 10 & 11 July being for horses, and 8 & 9 November for cattle and the hiring of farm staff. Originally held in Briggate, they were causing such great congestion by the late nineteenth century that new sites had to be found. Here we see a Leeds Fair being held around 1900, on land off Camp Road. By now the horses and cattle had disappeared, and it was simply a fun-fair complete with magnificent steam-driven carousels and a range of side-shows. Note the barefoot boys on the far right.

'The Feast often commences with Sabbath-breaking, money is uselessly spent and time wasted, — what drunkenness, and, in consequence thereof, sudden deaths, — what cursing and swearing, what licentiousness of conduct in other ways it produces'. This was Robert Jowitt's opinion of Woodhouse Feast in 1834, a view not shared by the local populace, for whom the Easter and late September feasts were virtually the only holidays they could enjoy throughout the entire working year. Further attempts to close the feast were made in 1913, but these were equally unsuccessful, and the feast continues to be held on Woodhouse Moor with the same popularity it had in the 1950s, when this photograph was taken.

The Paramount formed an important part of the new Headrow development, the architect Frank Verity providing an auditorium to hold 2,590 people behind Sir Reginald Blomfield's brick and Portland stone frontage to the Headrow and New Briggate. The opening night, 22 February 1932, was a splendid affair commencing with the *1812 Overture* performed by an orchestra seated before a scene of Moscow, complete with falling snow, and finishing with Rex O'Grady playing *On Ilkla Moor Baht 'At* on the £20,000 Wurlitzer organ. In 1940 this cinema changed its name to 'The Odeon', as it is still known today.

In 1874, Leeds Parish Church formed a recreation club which played cricket in summer and football in winter on its ground at Clarence Field. The parish magazine of 1879 'congratulated the players upon the increased skill displayed by them in the Rugby game, the improvement both in passing and dribbling being very great'. They had just beaten the town team in Keighley. At this time they were playing such local teams as St Andrew's, Hunslet Albion, Hunslet Excelsior and Leeds Imperial Rovers. Here the team poses outside one of the south doors of the Parish Church.

It is a hot July day in 1916, and, having finished their game of cricket, this amateur team now pose for their group photograph. Meanwhile, in the tent behind, all the cruets, neatly folded napkins and plates of food are being prepared for a splendid afternoon tea. It looks like a good sporting occasion, but in fact it records the Leeds City Parks Committee's inspection of their facilities at Roundhay.

The opening of the Leeds Cricket, Football & Athletic Co's new cricket ground on 27 May 1890, was a very successful event, 5,000 people attending to watch a match between Leeds and Scarborough. The Yorkshire County Cricket Club played its first match here in June 1891, a friendly with Derbyshire which it lost by 45 runs. The first County Championship game was played

here against Kent two months later and the first Test match, against Australia, in 1899. Ever since those times, Headingley has been the headquarters of Yorkshire CCC. Here a crowd watches a match with great interest in the opening years of this century.

Walter Farquhar Hook (1798-1875) was Vicar of Leeds from 1837 to 1859. A man of enormous energy and ability, he completely reformed religious life in the parish. The parish church itself was totally rebuilt, the quality of its music enhanced beyond recognition, the number of churches raised from eight to thirty-six and the schools increased from three to thirty. In addition, he persuaded the Corporation to purchase Woodhouse Moor as a public park, arbitrated in the strike of local colliers and, in all, made a truly memorable contribution to the future well-being of Leeds. Here we see him enjoying a pleasant afternoon in the cloisters of Kirkstall Abbey during a return visit to Leeds, when he was Dean of Chichester. He stands in the centre of the group, somewhat portly and wearing the traditional gaiters.

In 1881, the great Victorian Prime Minister, W.E.Gladstone, came to Leeds to address a demonstration of the Liberal Party. By today's standards, the preparations for this event were monumental in scale, the local architect Thomas Ambler being commissioned to create this vast temporary building to stand within the courtyard of the Coloured Cloth Hall. Here it is seen with the tables laid ready to receive over two thousand people for a banquet the day before the actual meeting took place. This was one of the first major electric lighting schemes in Leeds. Unfortunatley it failed halfway through, while the gaslights proved their reliability by continuing to burn throughout the meeting.

On 6 October 1894, the Hon Mrs E.C.Meynell Ingram entertained Their Royal Highnesses the Duke and Duchess of York at a splendid house party at Temple Newsam, the event being commemorated in this formal group taken before the entrance porch. The royal couple occupy the right-hand side of the doorway, close to Mrs Meynell Ingram and her favourite dog Valleta.

This fountain was first erected in the Fish Market, where its 'various squirts of all shapes and sizes, all seemingly with the one desperate intention of drowning passers-by' caused such an outcry that the Corporation re-sited it in front of the Town Hall. Here 'The Squirt', as it was known, was equally unloved, being described as a 'forsaken tea-urn, with the tap at the top'. Here crowds pose in the sunshine in April 1902, as workmen begin to dismantle it for removal to the Corporation yard.

This photograph of 16 September 1903 records the formal presentation to the City Council of all the statuary in City Square. It also marked the effective completion of this large civic piazza on the site of the former Coloured Cloth Hall. This truly enlightened scheme had been largely promoted by Col W.T.Harding, Lord Mayor of Leeds in 1898-99. He had provided Sir Thomas Brock's magnificent equestrian statue of the Black Prince, as well as the figures of Dean Hook and Joseph Priestley.

These, together with Cllr Boston's gift of John Harrison, and R.Wainwright's gift of James Watt, and their accompanying electrolier nymphs 'Morn' and 'Even' formed an outstanding group of sculpture, particularly when seen in their original architectural setting of fine stone balustrades and paving. When visitors to Leeds came into City Square in 1903, they knew that they were entering a city of pride, taste and wealth.

To commemorate the long reign of Queen Victoria, the citizens of Leeds raised £8,000 to erect a memorial in Victoria Square, directly in front of the Town Hall. The large Portland stone pedestal bore three bronze figures modelled by George Frampton R.A., 'Peace' held a palm leaf and an orb symbolising the world, 'Industry' was a smith stripped to the waist, while over all sat Her Majesty wearing her crown and Coronation robes. The memorial was unveiled on 27 November 1905 by the Lord Mayor, Edwin Woodhouse. Regrettably the taste for civic sculpture did not continue into the post-war years and so the Victoria Memorial was removed to Woodhouse Moor in 1937.

In the days before the National Health Service, private sponsorship and fund-raising events provided valuable income to support the local hospitals. The major annual event was the Hospital Fund Parade, part of which is shown here around 1905. Crowds line the upper part of North Street, the hotel with the clock-tower on the right fronting Tommy Green's engineering works. At this point the fire-brigade is riding by on one of their engines, their helmets glistening in the sun. Behind, in the low carriage, Superintendant Henry Richard Baker is seen wearing a peaked cap, while their fire-escape brings up the rear.

It is 4 January 1907, there have been heavy falls of snow over the past few days and so these lads, presumably with some adult help, have decided to build this igloo near Topcliffe Lane. The snow lacks its usual brilliant whiteness, and has taken on a distinct grey tone due to the pollution from hundreds of factory chimneys and thousands of household fires.

'Yorkshire's Loyal Welcome, The King and Queen greeted with enthusiasm — drizzling rain fails to damp the spirits of the crowd; the Lord Mayor of Leeds knighted.' These headlines described the visit of Edward VII and Alexandra to Leeds on 7 July 1908. In East Parade, as in other parts of the processional route, were 'clusters of green and gold, of scarlet and bright yellow, of red, of white, of blue, and festoons of real flowers from the garden and from the wild which contrasted effectively with the flowers of coloured paper'. The city had reason to celebrate, for it was the first visit by an English King for 262 years, and the last one had only come here by force!

Leeds suffragettes attending a rally on Woodhouse Moor in 1913. This photograph comes from the album of one of Leeds' most militant suffragettes, Leonora Cohen. According to an interview which she gave in 1938, these meetings on Woodhouse and Hunslet Moors were attended by crowds numbering 100,000 people.

Mrs Cohen, one of a small but vociferous group of active suffragettes in Leeds, was one of Mrs Pankhurst's bodyguards and achieved international notoriety in 1912, when she threw an iron bar through a jewel case in the Tower of London. She was again arrested at this rally, on a charge of inciting rebellion, and again later in 1913, when a visit of Prime Minister Asquith to Leeds saw an outbreak of militant suffragette actions in the city.

The outbreak of World War One in 1914 saw a truce between the suffragettes and the Government, and the end to militant activity. Women over thirty were given the vote in 1918. Mrs Cohen became active in trade union work, was appointed a Leeds magistrate in 1922, and was awarded the OBE for public services in 1928.

This exhibit of 'a reconstructed crash indicating the fate of an enemy machine after its last fatal nose-dive to earth' formed part of the Royal Air Force Exhibition opened in three temporary hangers in Roundhay Park in May 1919. This exhibition showed a variety of British, Austrian and German 'planes, aircraft engines, a mobile workshop, an anti-aircraft gunnery station and a balloon section. In addition, the crowds were entertained by spectacular flying demonstrations by 'the world's greatest pilots'. In the days before television, exhibitions of this type played an important part of popular education in Leeds.

Above: It is Saturday, 2 May 1914 and after weeks of planning, this four-wheeled cart, its occupants and its horse have all been prepared for the colourful procession along Town Street where, with luck, it might win one of the special prizes. Hours of hard work have gone into making the costumes, arranging the floral decorations and Japanese lanterns, grooming the horse, and polishing every piece of its harness and brasses. It is all in a very good cause, however, for in addition to providing everyone with a really enjoyable day, Bramley Carnival also raised welcome funds for the Leeds General Infirmary.

Left: At the end of World War One, a War Memorial Executive Committee was established to raise the necessary funds to erect an appropriate memorial to the city's dead. A site in Cookridge Street was selected and a scheme prepared by Sir Reginald Blomfield. However, in 1921 the committee invited Col T.W.Harding to prepare an alternative version and so, working with the London sculptor H.C.Fehr, he prepared the designs for this monument, which was unveiled in City Square on 14 October 1922. The figure of Winged Victory hovers above Peace, in the form of a female figure bearing an olive branch, and War, shown as St George slaying the dragon. As traffic congestion increased, the memorial was later re-sited on the Headrow's Garden of Rememberance.

On the outbreak of war in 1939, air-raid shelters were rapidly constructed for both communal and family use, the latter being either dug into the garden or created within a basement area.

This photograph, taken on 15 October 1940, shows a very comfortable basement shelter, probably at 11 Cardinal Avenue. The gasmasks hang ready for use on the left-hand wall.

Compared to most great industrial centres, Leeds suffered very little damage from wartime bombing. The popular reason for this, and one which is probably true, is that the permanent pall of black, sulphrous smoke which hung over the city up to the introduction of clean-air policies, made Leeds virtually invisible during night-time air-raids. During the second air-raid on Leeds, on the evening of 31 August 1941, the Marsh Lane Goods Station received a direct hit. A *Yorkshire Evening News* journalist was in a nearby street at the time. He reported: *"Better take cover,"*

the warden said, "he's just dropped a salvo over there." His words were followed by the shrill 'wheee' of falling bombs which exploded not far away. Fire-fighting units worked fiercely while armed soldiers stood by with the British Tommies' derisive cheerfulness when 'things are happening'. From the entrance to the public air-raid shelter nearby came the sounds: "Let's have a barrel of fun . . ." It was dawn when I reached home, so I breakfasted rather earlier than usual. Air-raids do one thing with unfailing regularity. They make me hungry.'

On Saturday, 15 March 1941, a German bomber dropped a series of bombs on Leeds city centre, one making a direct hit on the City Museum and another blasting through the north-east corner of the Town Hall. At the museum, John Wilson, the foreman porter, was saved by his steel helmet and a door which was blown on top of him, diverting the falling debris, and fortunately no one was seriously injured. The same could not be said of the collections, however, a number of Egyptian mummies, Greek pottery, birds and animals being totally destroyed. It took the Curator and his staff some weeks to sift through all the rubble in order to recover the fine collections of coins, medals and archaeological specimens.

In November 1941, shortly after the City Council had decided to adopt the aircraft-carrier *HMS Ark Royal*, she was sunk off Gibralter. As part of War Savings Week in 1942, the city of Leeds set itself the target of £5 million, but this sum almost doubled, some £9.3 million being raised. Some of this was in savings, but crowds of people also queued outside the Civic Hall to deliver their personal gifts into the Lord Mayor's office. In this photograph we see General De Gaulle, leader of the Free French Forces, taking the salute at the march-past of Allied troops in the Ark Royal Week parade on 6 May 1942.

VE Day, 8 May 1945, and the war in Europe was over. The whole of Leeds celebrated as never before — or since. Singing and cheering crowds thronged the city centre, filling Victoria Square and clambering on to the Town Hall's lions. In the suburbs, street parties commenced with necessarily sparse tea-parties in the open air, followed by bonfires and singing after dark. This crowd of women and children, with only three men, reflects the joy and relief that everyone felt on this occasion.

SUBSCRIBERS

Presentation Copies

1 Councillor Denise Atkinson, Lord Mayor of Leeds
2 Councillor Jon Trickett. Leader of Leeds City Council
3 Councillor Bernard Atha, Chairman, Cultural Services Committee
4 Councillor Christiana Myers, Chairman, Museums Sub-Committee
5 Leeds City Museums • 6 Leeds City Libraries
7 P.C.D.Brears, Dip.AD, FSA, FMA

8 Martin Jarred	53 Joan Newiss	97 John Stuart Aspinall
9 John H José	54 David Patchett	98 John Hird
10 Mr & Mrs Ernest Johnston	55 Mollie E Barber	99 R S Howard
11 Mr & Mrs John Gall	56 Brian Eastwood	100 Mrs Margaret Wood
12 Mr & Mrs Mel Philipson	57 Joyce Laughlin	101 Geoffrey Firth
13 Mr & Mrs Stephen Harrison	58 Pauline Askwith	102 Christopher Gowland
14 Mr & Mrs H Houghton	59 Martin K Spreadbury	Green
15 Mr & Mrs J Malden	60 Derek Franks	103 Gisella Dyson
16 Mr & Mrs Mike Loynd	61 Mr M Doherty	104 Gisella Dyson
17 Norman Scawthorn	62 Margaret Coates	105 Eric Triffitt
18 Dennis Williamson	63 Stanley Newport	106 Barbara Nichols
19 Harold Sutcliffe	64 Mr A S Chapman	107 Norman Frank Powell
20 Dr K A Mountfort	65 Barrie Dennison	108 Mr W J Prichard
21 Mr A G Harrison BSc ACII	66 Denis Mason Jones	109 Harry Taylor
22 Edna Marjorie Lythe	67 Leonard Dean	110 Tony and Pat Wilson
23 Ivon Tirson	68 Mrs Margaret King	111 Brian Bedford
24 Roy Townend	69 Mr William Edward	112 Peter John Cunnane
25 Gladys Jordan	Cowling	113 Debra and Stephen Missett
26 Peter G Buckland	70 Thomas Griffin	114 Horace Hodgson
27 Fred Bickerdike	71 Tom Rainford	115 Kenneth Knott
28 Derek Thwaites	72 Denis William Coe	116 G I Friedman
29 Eric K Darley	73 Mildred Bertha Carter	117 Raymond J Woodcraft
30 Jane Margaret Cox	74 Sandra L Smith	118 Gerald H Green
31 D G Bridge	75 Victoria C Maxhara	119 Joan Ramell
32 Miss Nelly Sutcliffe	76 Mr E I Kendrew	120 Marian Craddock
33 Pamela Mack	77 Mrs Eileen Smith	121 Laurence Tyers
34 Jack E Walker	78 Theresa Spellman	122 Mrs Ann Clark
35 John Lowrey	79 Mrs Norma Dixon	123 E H Newman
36 Mrs Molly Rodley	80 Miss Bronwyn White	124 Geoffrey Arthur Fish
37 Jane Marshall	81 Kenneth Mitchell	125 L R Whyte
38 Edwin Leuty	82 Richard Sanderson	126 Frank Hickling
39 Mr J Gavins	83 Peter Brennan	127 B Cavell
40 Ian Pearson	84 May Jeffrey	128 Mr George Atack
41 J D Barker	85 Peter Cross	129 D B Palmer
42 Richard J White	86 Eunice Gray	130 Mr & Mrs J O Wolfe
43 Linda Biran	87 Margaret Smith	131 Mr & Mrs R Fish
44 Mrs Elaine Briggs	88 Terence Martin Pacey	132 Frank Coggill
45 S M C Tomlinson	89 Anthony Silson	133 Alun Pugh
46 Kevin Brown	90 Myrtle Young	134 John and Mary Myers
47 A Gillon	91 R E Redman	135 Mrs B J Forster
48 L E Walker	92 Jack Furness	136 Shirley Heald
49 Jennifer M Eastwood	93 Mr & Mrs K Booth	137 Mrs Mavis Ivatts
50 Rowland Thackray	94 Mrs Margaret Smith	138 J Lamb
51 Eric Cavell	95 Peter Westerman	139 Sylvia E Harris
52 Ann-Marie Farrar	96 Peter Place	140 Jeffrey Harris

141 Doug Walker
142 D Brown
143 Betty and Harry Winston
144 Betty and Harry Winston
145 Phillip Mark Pearson
146 David Hunter
147 Mrs Judy C Marno
148 Mr Norman C Lowe
149 Lawrence Keough
150 Gordon Mawman
151 H Clarkson
152 J D & E Hall
153 Peter & June Jones
154 Barry Bellhouse
155 Elizabeth Minkin

156 Michael J Passman
157 Stuart Anslow
158 Muriel Greaves
159 E M Baker
160 Mr G B Roberts
161 Robert Gibson
162 Brian Smith
163 Peter & Sylvia Everett
164 Charles F Brownridge
165 Christine M Fenton
166 H W Adkin
167 Mr J C Revie
168 Brenda M Bentham
169 Leslie Collinson
170 Elizabeth French

171 Margaret A Marks
172 Michael Hoggett
173 Dr David A Furniss
174 Tom Jarrett
175 Jean Lawson
176 R Brian Roberts
177 Rowena Rice
178 Mrs Kathleen Metcalf
179 Roy and Pauline Tulloch
180 A A Jackson
181 Jean Hagan
182 A Warburton
183 Mrs Edna Collard
184 G C Fowler
185 Patricia Mary Evans